What Judith's Clients Say

'Theologian, kinesiologist, spiritual advisor and so much more, Judith McAdam has transformed the lives of those who have crossed paths with this healing muse and lodestar. She is like a guiding star, revealing the path to reaching your full potential.'
DEARBHAIL MCDONALD, AUTHOR AND BROADCASTER

'Judith is a modern-day Sherpa, lovingly guiding people along the mountain track towards the life that has always been waiting for them.'
KATHY SCOTT, THE TRAILBLAZERY

'Judith has a priceless wisdom. Every soul she encounters is set on a path of discovering their true self, true purpose and inner authentic power.'
NADINE QUINN AND CARLA MCQUILLAN, THE SPACE

'When I first met Judith, I was meandering along a lonely path of general distraction to fulfil the empty space. As far as I am concerned I attribute most of my newfound happiness and unique family situation to Judith's indelible guidance.'
BRIGID O'HORA, MOTHER OF TRIPLETS

'Judith guides you to the answers you already have inside, unlocking fears and breaking patterns. Her methods have helped me to understand how I hold the power to align myself to create whatever it is I seek, both personally and professionally.'
KATE VERLING, MINK HAND & FOOT SPA

'Judith has a very special gift. Her methods are remarkable and they have been truly helpful in both my personal and professional life.'
AIMEE HART, DIRECTOR, TIME DATA SECURITY

'Judith's method has helped me overcome personal problems and grow in confidence and self-love. When you apply her methods to your life the outcomes are amazing!'
EMMA KEHOE

'I would describe Judith's work as a miracle and a gift to any life she touches. She is a teacher, confidante and an angel on earth. I can't imagine how different my life would be had I not met Judith.'
ASHLEY KEHOE

'Judith is warmth and counsel, nurturing energy and grounding wisdom. She is earth mother and soul sister; she is the truth you didn't want to hear and the answer to your prayers. I'm incredibly grateful that Judith is part of my life and my story, that she enabled me to love myself wholly, to let the light in, and then shine that light out to everyone in my life.'
ANDREW HYLAND, FORMER DIRECTOR, MARRIAGE EQUALITY

The Source

Connect with your inner power and
create your own reality

JUDITH McADAM

GILL BOOKS

Gill Books

Hume Avenue

Park West

Dublin 12

www.gillbooks.ie

Gill Books is an imprint of M.H. Gill and Co.

© Judith McAdam 2018

978 07171 8125 4

Designed by www.grahamthew.com

Edited by Jane Rogers

Proofread by Ellen Christie

Printed by CPI Group (UK) Ltd, Croydon CRO 4YY

This book is typeset in FreightText Pro 9.5 on 17pt .

The paper used in this book comes from the wood pulp of managed
forests. For every tree felled, at least one tree is planted, thereby
renewing natural resources.

5 4 3 2 1

Acknowledgements

To Cathal, Cillian and Clodagh – your encouragement and love fills the pages of this book. Deep appreciation to my mother Val, father Jim, brother Darren and all my family – you are the bedrock of my world. To my dear friends, Carmel Howard, Delma Gallagher, Gabrielle Prendeville, John Laing, Mags Wilki, Joseph Casey and Lisa Hyland, thank you from my heart. Much love and appreciation to Andrew Hyland and Kellie O'Rourke, you are powerful beacons of light. Thanks to perhaps the finest visionaries in Ireland, Kathy Scott, Ruth Meehan, Lydia Campbell and Teresa Daly for their expertise and faith in me. Thanks to Commissioning Editor Sarah Liddy, Editor Sheila Armstrong, Jamie O'Connell and all at Gill Books. Thanks to Doreen Kilfeather, Peter Homan, Fiona Cribben, Sara White and White Bear Design – you are brilliant creators. Thanks to Sean Beakey for Amatsu. Thanks to Ashley O'Rourke, Sam Taylor, Carla Hartnett, Darina O'Rourke, Anna-Louise O'Donovan, Sarah Dunleavy, Victoria McCormack, Nadine Quinn, Anna Fahy, Liz Prunty, Billie Grogan, Robert McCann, Gearoid and Angela Hardy and families – your energy is in the foundations of this book. To all those I have deep connections with, you know who you are, and to Val, Mary and Wayne for looking after me from the other side.

Finally, to each person who comes to me, my sincere love and thanks. I speak to your heart individually when I say you are my inspiration. I am truly privileged to walk some of your journey with you and to see you step into your personal and higher purpose in this life. I bow my head to you, Anam Cara.

To Cathal, Cillian and Clodagh
you are where the divine and human meet
so play all your life in the field of pure potential.

The Promise

It is possible to DELIBERATELY CREATE
what you desire in life.

There are people actually doing it ALL THE TIME.

You are an INTEGRAL PART OF THE UNIVERSE and have
access to infinite intelligence constantly.

You have an energetic, mental and emotional reality and
NOT JUST A PHYSICAL REALITY.

Within you is where THE DIVINE AND HUMAN MEET.

This union between the divine and human within is where
YOUR DESIRES ARE CONCEIVED.

Your desires are nurtured in your mind and are borne out
into PHYSICAL REALITY.

You have a PERSONAL PURPOSE and a HIGHER PURPOSE
in this lifetime.

You are continuously CHANNELLING ENERGY.

EVERYTHING YOU WANT is available to you.

You just need to know HOW TO ACCESS IT.

This is THE PROMISE.

Come follow me, I WILL SHOW YOU HOW ...

Introduction

SEVEN YEARS AGO on a very cold and wet April day I found myself journeying from Mayo back to my native Dublin. I had lived in Spain for a few years before moving to Mayo, and the drive from Mayo to Dublin was one I had done many times. But this time, it was the beginning of my journey home – not only to Dublin, but more importantly, the journey home to myself. I was leaving Mayo and I was terrified. It was pelting down and the windscreen wipers were trying desperately to clear the fogged-up window. The miserable weather echoed the desperation and desolation I felt deep within me. The boot of my car was jam packed with plastic bags and a suitcase and in the back seat were my thirteen-year-old twin boys and my beautiful seven-year-old daughter. I remember thinking: 'All I need is in this car, my children and the real me – that's all I need.'

I was a divorced forty-one-year-old woman with no money, no job, nowhere to live, on my way back to my parents' house. I was on my own internal pilgrimage. I had come too far away from my real self. I had been afraid to listen to and act on my own intuition and now I had finally stripped my life bare only to begin anew. I was responsible for that and now I had to rebuild my life with one major difference: it was going to be in accordance with who I really was and not who I thought I should be or what society dictated to me.

The emergence

—

I desperately tried to find my feet in those early days of despair. I had beaten myself up badly and on arriving back in Dublin I was very broken. I had to start from absolute scratch. This had been my choice, so it had to be my own journey back to me. But I didn't really know where to begin. My children were my priority, so there were schools to find, new uniforms and books to buy. I had to rent a house and move in. More importantly, I needed to put food on the table – and I had no job. Thankfully, I did have loving support from family and friends, but ultimately this was my life and I had to take responsibility for it. Over the years I had not been true to myself and now I had decided to turn it all around. 'What doesn't kill you will make you stronger' so they say, but boy did it nearly kill me. My children settled in quickly and were enjoying Dublin, but for me those first few months were terrifying. I felt like I was a shadow of myself and I worried constantly about money. Everything rolled around in my head endlessly and that incessant fearful chatter was unceasing. To make matters worse, it was in the middle of the recession and it seemed like the whole of Dublin was erupting at the seams with money worries.

But one of the positive things that comes from being a mother with three children and stripping your life bare is that you really can't afford to procrastinate. I just had to start putting my life back together again. However this time I was listening to my intuition and my intuition was loudly telling me to re-open my practice. I had been a kinesiologist, reiki practitioner and reflexologist many years before my travels and now I found myself at the bottom of the stairs in my rented house throwing my hands up to heaven and saying out loud, 'Okay, I will do what you want me to do, just make it easy.' I was at my wits' end and had finally stopped going against my inner knowing. I had no choice. I conceded and with that I took the first step and I got a loan of a therapy couch.

I decorated the back room of my rented house, all the time coaxing myself to move forward inch by inch, and sometimes centimetre by centimetre. I got business cards and, finally, I got one lovely client. Step by step I began to deliberately create my own reality. Don't get me wrong – I had loads and loads of wobbles and moments when I was nearly riveted to the spot with fear. But I was following my intuition. I was using my gifts and allowing Source Energy to flow through me as best I could. I surrendered to that infinitely intelligent energy and that's exactly what it proved to be – infinitely intelligent. It knew what it was doing even if I didn't. My business began to flourish and my house became like Grand Central station. So I moved my practice to another building and it was during those seven years that the seven principles of deliberately creating unfolded. In those years I have allowed myself to become like a beautiful butterfly.

I went back to college myself and completed a four-year honours degree in theology. My business has developed to such a degree that I now run workshops and seminars helping others to deliberately create what they want in their own lives. I have also raised my wonderful children. My twin sons are in college and my daughter is thriving in secondary school.

In my case I am now being led into my higher purpose, which involves writing this book. In the last seven years I have completely opened myself up to this wonderful Source Energy, which is at the heart of all creation. I have aligned myself with it. I feel like the caterpillar that has come out of the chrysalis. Now this is my promise: I *will* do the same for you.

The promise I made to myself

—

This promise that I make you to is one that I have made to myself first. I know you can deliberately create your own reality, creating all that you want in life. No matter what it is – a new car, a relationship, a change of career – I know you can fulfil your personal purpose and also your higher purpose. I know this is all possible, because I am doing it and I teach others to do it too. I know the seven practices in this book work because I developed and emerged through them. I clambered out of my unawareness, sometimes ungracefully and more times than not causing mayhem on the way. If you compare me to a caterpillar and the metaphorical transformation into a butterfly, I was the caterpillar that completely resisted the transfiguration. I kicked and screamed, trying to hang on to all that wasn't working in my life out of fear. I was afraid to let go, afraid to grow. I was actually afraid of something awful happening in my life if that metamorphosis did take place, and I was absolutely terrified of becoming that beautiful butterfly.

These seven practices were borne out of my suffering, a suffering which needed never to have taken place had I been more aware of who I really was. But magically my pain has also been transformed by these seven principles. Alchemy has taken place and all the suffering has turned to gold. You don't have to go to the terrifying extremes that I did; I have already paved the way for you. All you have to do is follow these seven principles that I have developed from being out there at the coal face.

I was expecting you, you are welcome

—

When people walk through the door of my practice they think they are entering as strangers, but not to me. Unbeknownst to them, they have already created their visit in the recesses of their minds and by the time they are standing in front of me it is being borne out into reality. I have honed my craft and have the ability to see their pure potential. It is their higher self that arrives to me eager to be recognised and released. Their intuition has led them to me and they have listened to that soft voice that whispers constantly inside them.

They are instinctively drawn to me because they are ready to unleash their pure potential, to release that *big* person that lies within. They are now ready to ripple from the inside out.

Sometimes when we look into the mirror we only see ourselves through our generational conditioning. Life is filtered through our old wounds and fears. For the large part we are in unawareness of this and we create our reality based on this distorted reflection.

When people make their connection with me they are ready to enter the mystical realm of deliberately creating their own reality, ready to mindfully create what they want in their lives. This is because they are starting to see themselves as multidimensional. They recognise their physical reality is only *one* part and not the *whole* of 'who they really are'. They are willing to see the real reflection of themselves, to see their glorious, unbounded, limitless self. Then they start to reflect this abundance in their physical reality.

Metaphorically speaking, by opening this book and starting to read it you have just 'walked though my door.' The door you have opened leads into the deep chasm of your subconscious mind, into a magical, mystical world of imagination, visualisation and creation. You will be tuning your own mind into the field of pure potential and aligning with the one-mind of this magnificent energy.

I have studied many world religions and these mystical, spiritual experiences are a common thread between all of them; the common denominator, so to speak. Over centuries these spiritual experiences have been given names and associations with God, Yahweh, Allah, the Holy Spirit, the universe – the list is endless. For example, Yahweh, Allah or God has also been associated with maleness. Language can be laden with negative connotations, deeply colouring our perception. So within these pages it is my wish to transcend the outdated image of a patriarchal God and to speak a universal language everyone will understand. The words that I use to describe this powerful energy that infuses every living thing is *Source Energy*. You will be using this powerful, limitless energy that courses through your human veins to conjure up feeling, create momentum and manifest your own abundant reality, while grounding this reality into the physical world you live in. In other words creating what you want in your life abundantly.

Believe it or not, you are an energetic conduit for Source Energy. This energy works in you, for you and through you. You are constantly connected to Source Energy, otherwise you would not exist. You are continually channelling this energy and you have access to this at all times, whether you realise it or not. Your physical reality is only one part of you – your energetic reality comes first, as this is where your desires are conceived. Your mental and emotional reality incubates your desires, while your physical reality is simply the outer manifestation of what has been going on internally. The key to manifesting what you want in life is to know 'who you really are' and master the art of accessing all of these aspects of you.

Be under no illusion: you have asked for big change and now you are receiving the information you need to make those changes. So don't resist it through fear. Don't be afraid of new language or new ideas that sometimes may take a while to process. At the beginning it might seem hard to get your head around some of these concepts, but you will settle into it very quickly. As human beings, we often ask and it is given, but then we run for the hills with fear. Remember you are being guided from within. If you are reading this, now you are ready for it. You are ready for big change, make no mistake about that. You can go as fast or as slowly as you like, it is up to you. Just don't deny it, fight it or procrastinate, instead accept it and get excited at the many wonders that lie within you that you haven't tapped into yet – but you will.

Now let us prepare the way energetically and meet your own inner child ...

Judith

PART ONE

Preparing the Way

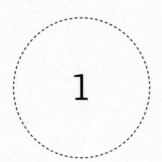

1

Creating
Your Comfort
Zone

IN THIS CHAPTER I will be creating a comfort zone for you. This snug, safe space is more relevant than you think. It is really important that you are relaxed. Because when you tune yourself in, you align your own mind to the one-mind of Source Energy. This is necessary to create the changes you wish for in your life. In this calmed state the portal or doorway between Source Energy and you opens up, normally through the crown chakra. This allows you to access the field of pure potential. This is where the divine and human meet. Wouldn't it be lovely to be fully aligned with this energy connecting you to unconditional love, personal power, strength, limitlessness and abundance of health, wealth, joy and happiness? You can really do this and your comfort zone will gradually make way for it to happen, allowing you to gently leave behind the stresses and strains of the material world, ultimately creating whatever you want in your life.

What you will learn from each chapter

—

To give you an insight into what to expect from each chapter there will be a paragraph on 'what you will learn' to help you tune into Source Energy. Your expectations are crucial in the process of creating your own reality. If you can't feel, expect and think it, you can't create it. It is essential to place soft focus on your expectations, as they positively influence your subconscious mind. Your subconscious mind has a very important part to play in deliberately creating your own reality. Thankfully, your subconscious loves imagination, intuition and creativity, so in each chapter you will be connecting to and using these powerful tools.

On this journey you will be meeting Andrew, Kellie and me, ordinary people who are creating extraordinary lives. We share our stories here as examples of what is possible.

Throughout the book I use metaphors to help provide clarity. The kite metaphor is one of my favourites and particularly useful, so I will touch on that in this chapter.

There are two important characters in this book: one of them is Source Energy; the other, who profoundly influences your life, is your own inner child. This child lies deep in the recesses of your subconscious mind. Without the co-operation of this inner child you will find it very hard, if not impossible, to move forward. This is a big concept, which I will explain in detail in these pages, but for now trust me and let the journey begin.

The seven principles

—

In this book, I offer you the seven principles I applied to my own life. They can work for anything you desire: a family, a relationship, success in business, a holiday in the sun. These principles lead you to fulfil your personal purpose. Then when your basic human needs are being met you are free to pursue your higher purpose in life.

1 **CONNECT TO SOURCE ENERGY:** Acknowledging who you really are and embracing the fact that you are inextricably linked to infinite intelligence and are part of the field of pure potential.

2 **ALIGNMENT:** Building a relationship with your inner child and tuning yourself into Source Energy and your desires.

3 **FEELING AND KNOWING:** Using your intuition and creating positive loops in your life.

4 **DECISIONS AND EXPECTATIONS:** Making *f*ck it* decisions and becoming consciously aware of the power of positive choices.

5 **MOMENTUM:** Stepping through your fears and consciously creating positive momentum.

6 **RECEIVING:** Ask and it is given – receiving spiritually, mentally, emotionally and physically.

7 **RETURN TO SOURCE ENERGY:** Staying aligned, accessing your personal and higher purpose and the collective consciousness.

These seven principles will give you everything you need to create your own reality.

Creating your comfort zone

—

Now let me help you to create your comfort zone and prepare the way for you to receive the information in these pages. This is your time; you are giving yourself space to develop your own awareness, and this is the first step. Be patient – sometimes you need to slow down to go faster.

We'll start by energetically connecting you with your own five senses; sight, hearing, touch, smell and taste. You are a very intuitive human being and getting more closely in touch with your senses allows you to tune in and pick up the subtle signs and intuitions available to us all the time. This will also make the information held in these pages more accessible to you. You are working not only with your conscious mind but with your subconscious as well.

Here's a brief example of how you can tune into this subtle energy.

Recently a young man came to me whose mother had just died. He was distraught, and after his session I was writing down his next appointment date and some notes on a piece of paper for him. I had run out of paper earlier that morning, so I searched through a pile of pages I had kept aside for children to colour on. I wrote his instructions on the back of one of these pages and handed it to him. I apologised for the infantile picture on the back of the page. When he looked at the picture, he began to cry. It was a lovely big drawing of a butterfly. He said that earlier that morning, his aunt had told him that his mother would come to him with butterflies. He had tuned himself into this and was ready to receive a butterfly – and he did.

Many imaginative tools will be offered to you during the course of our time together. These tools are essential in helping you to relax and deliberately create. Just for a few minutes I would like you to start developing your own tools in awareness. You will begin by using them every time you sit down to read this book. Then eventually you will bring them into all aspects of your life. These tools are comforting and will be a joy to use. You will be able to tap into this field of pure potential and it is much easier to do this if you are relaxed.

If you were sitting in my therapy rooms I would be using aromatherapy oils, and perhaps you would like to do the same. For example, lavender oil is really calming. While you read, use the oil to soothe you into a deeper sense of relaxation. Perhaps you could sprinkle the oil on your book – this is a lovely thing to do, and it will gently nourish you each time you sit to read – or simply burn some incense. There is method in my madness. Just for now, trust me.

'Ask and it will be given to you; seek and you will find; knock and the door will be opened to you.'

MATTHEW 7:7

Now get a photograph of yourself when you were a child and put it beside you. Look at how beautiful you were. Can you see the magic in your young eyes? Let the photo of this lovely child be your reading companion. Connect with the child in the picture. Light a candle and watch it flickering while you wrap yourself up in a cosy blanket and listen to the sound of your breath. You are very safe and just for these moments really feel and know that. You have deliberately created a comfort zone for yourself. There is nothing for you to do. Have a steaming hot cuppa beside you and know that this is the beginning of your exciting journey into deliberately creating your own reality.

From now on let our oils, candles, blankets and photo become tools in your ever-growing toolbox. You are already developing your awareness bit by bit. It doesn't take long.

Your travelling companions

—

Now I'd like you to meet Andrew and Kellie and welcome them into your heart. They are brave pioneers who, along with me, will be opening themselves up to you so that you can see how we have created our own reality using the processes I have developed and outlined in this book. Each of us has our very own unique set of gifts, which, coupled with our own deep and compelling desires, we make manifest in our lives.

Andrew has a very big energy presence. He is an admirable man with two deep desires for equality and unconditional love; desires that he simply had to make manifest in his reality. He was the co-director of Marriage Equality and a founder and director of communications for Yes Equality, the organisation created to campaign for a yes vote in the marriage equality referendum in Ireland in 2015. Andrew was an integral part of a magnificent collective consciousness, which would go on to inspire a paradigm shift throughout the world. Ireland became the first country to vote for same-sex marriage. In just one generation Ireland had shifted from an overwhelmingly conservative mindset on sexuality to a transformational view that influenced the world. Andrew was a co-creator in this great change. He will share with you his experiences in deliberately creating his own change throughout the campaign using the steps outlined in this book.

I've heard people describe Kellie as 'effortlessly cool and relaxed'. Kellie is vivacious and embodies a beautiful sense of freedom. She demonstrates how you can turn your negative experiences into liquid gold if you hold steady and align yourself. Kellie developed post-traumatic stress after a car accident in Australia, followed by a difficult court case. Kellie had two main desires when she came back from Australia after the accident. One was to 'fix' herself and the other was to work in the music business. Using the steps in this book, and after finding herself in some fairly negative situations, she went on to create a job working for one of the biggest rock bands in the world and going on tour with them. She is also going to share her story with you.

For my own part I will explore two of my deep compelling desires. One is to become self-actualised, to fulfil my potential as a woman. I want to go beyond the limits society dictates to me. The second is a desire for a transcendent level of knowledge. I am deliberately creating my own reality, while going beyond a patriarchal God.

The three of us are very different people with contrasting desires. Each one of us has come into this life with an energetic blueprint of what we want to create; our own unique potential, our needs, wants and desires.

It really doesn't matter what you wish to create in your life: there is no specification, no rights or wrongs and no criteria. This is your life and you are completely free to create what you wish – health, love, family, equality, or a fantastic career, money, travelling the world, a new car – it really doesn't matter. Your master plan is particular to you and you are allowed to have it.

The kite metaphor and your desires

—

Imagine standing in a green field on a summer day. The sun is shining and there is a soft warm breeze. Looking down at your hand you realise you are holding strings of kites. As you look up, notice that you can't see some of these kites. They are too far away. That doesn't matter. You feel happy because there are many kites now coming into your view. These are your kites. Each kite holds one of your deep desires. You have all the strings in your hand. These kites represent your creations. These desires could be for a lover, a child, more money or a better job. You might want to create a big project or a new business. It could be a desire to pass an exam or to create peace and joy in your life. In fact, becoming aligned with Source Energy ensures better health, wealth, joy and happiness. This is the natural state of being when you are aligned. This is the only state that matters. Everything else flows from there.

No matter what your desires are, you have the strings in your hand. At the moment you are putting soft focus on them. Know that they are there and you can bring them into land. Feel them around you. Feel your dreams and imaginings as little tugs on the strings in your hand. Feel and know that you can create them and bring them into being. You are using soft focus. It is a soft, gentle way to create without anxiety. For now just hold the strings and let all your kites bob easily in the sky. Visualise yourself running happily with all your wonderful kites.

The kite represents your desire and the string in your hand represents your connection to it. The moment you had the desire you formed a connection. That connection is irrevocable. The kite of your desire is getting ready to land in this physical reality.

Sometimes our desires are so long in coming we forget we even had the desire in the first place. Why, then, do we not create instantaneously? Well, we do, but only a shred of reality – the string – it needs to gather and grow. We block it from developing, mainly because of fear. We have become so good at it that we are unaware that we are doing it. Through generations of conditioning we have forgotten the art of deliberately creating and have lapsed into various degrees of unawareness. This is what blocks your kites from coming in to land.

The kite metaphor is very useful in feeling what stage your creations are at. It also develops your imagination and visualisation skills. You will be feeling your way around things. You are developing your feeling, knowing and intuition skills. Don't worry if you are out of practice. Just go with it.

At the end of this chapter, you are going to write down three of your desires. Everyone's desires are different – you might want to create more money, a loving partner, a child. For someone else it might be a promotion, a new house or a sense of purpose in life. While you go through each chapter keep your three desires in mind; see them in your mind's eye, bobbing like kites, visualise the strings in your hand. Do not concern yourself yet with how you are going to land these kites. Just allow yourself to play with the idea that it is possible. The most important thing is allowing yourself to think it.

As you absorb the information in this book, you will apply it to your kites and gently start to pull the strings masterfully in to land.

The chakra system

—

In my practice, I work with the chakra system, and at the beginning of each chapter I will be asking you to tune in to a particular one. Chakras are centres in the body where energy flows through, and I will be focusing on the seven main chakras. If you are not familiar with chakras, don't worry. Here is a brief explanation:

O The **CROWN CHAKRA** is found at the top of your head, and it connects you with Source Energy and the field of pure potential. It is associated with the colours white and violet.

O The **THIRD EYE CHAKRA** is found at the forehead in between the eyes. It is concerned with intuition, imagination, wisdom and decision making. It is associated with the colour indigo.

O The **THROAT CHAKRA** is located at the throat and is concerned with communication, self-expression and truth. It is associated with the colour blue.

O The **HEART CHAKRA** is found just above the area of the heart. It is concerned with love, joy and peace. It is associated with the colour green.

O The **SOLAR PLEXUS CHAKRA** is found above the navel. It is concerned with personal power, self-worth and confidence. It is associated with the colour yellow.

O The **SACRAL CHAKRA** is found about two inches below the navel. It is concerned with creativity, sensuality, sexuality and abundance. It is associated with the colour orange.

O The **ROOT CHAKRA** is found at the base of the spine and is concerned with survival issues, such as how you meet your basic human needs. It is associated with the colour red.

'Chakras are centres in the body
where energy flows through'

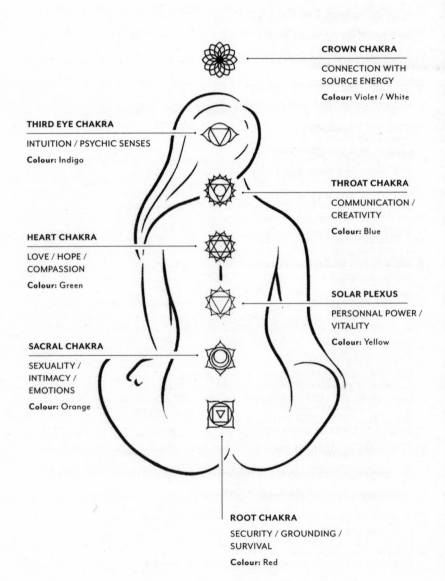

CROWN CHAKRA

CONNECTION WITH
SOURCE ENERGY

Colour: Violet / White

THIRD EYE CHAKRA

INTUITION / PSYCHIC SENSES

Colour: Indigo

THROAT CHAKRA

COMMUNICATION /
CREATIVITY

Colour: Blue

HEART CHAKRA

LOVE / HOPE /
COMPASSION

Colour: Green

SOLAR PLEXUS

PERSONNAL POWER /
VITALITY

Colour: Yellow

SACRAL CHAKRA

SEXUALITY /
INTIMACY /
EMOTIONS

Colour: Orange

ROOT CHAKRA

SECURITY / GROUNDING /
SURVIVAL

Colour: Red

Mantras and phrases

—

Throughout this book I will refer to certain phrases and mantras. This type of positive repetition influences your subconscious mind and helps you to conjure up feelings. I will be using the terms 'conscious mind' and 'subconscious mind' as opposed to the 'unconscious mind' traditionally used by psychologists and psychiatrists. I also use the term 'abundance', which represents health, wealth, joy and happiness. In each chapter there will be references to focus. Both soft and intense focus will be explored through imagination and visualisation. Your subconscious is used to you giving it mixed messages, so focus gives your subconscious clear direction, allowing you to create faster and more accurately. An example of one of the mantras I use frequently is 'just keep stepping, just keep stepping'. I use this for everything big and small. My daughter modified it over the years to 'just keep swimming, just keep swimming', mimicking the character of Dory from *Finding Nemo* – either way it is useful in reminding you to step through your fears.

Meditation

—

Meditation is your biggest tool for bridging the gap between you and the limitless energy of Source Energy, allowing you passage. It would be really helpful for you to create time for meditation in your life at some point. However, in times of trouble and crisis it can seem hard to do. Meditation isn't something we in the West have grown up with, so it is sometimes easier to bring yourself to it gently and gradually. Let me set this expectation for you now: you will lead yourself to meditation eventually.

All the meditations in this book are available for free on my website, www.judithmcadam.com.

Toolbox

—

I will be introducing you to tools and practices throughout this book to help support you on your way. At the end of each chapter I will give you a set of tools to put in your imaginary toolbox. These tools will be an essential part of your journey.

Imagine your life being like a game of chess. When you learn the rules of the game you can move your pieces around the board more thoughtfully and less randomly. We have been conditioned to look outside ourselves, so going inwards will take a little bit of practice, but it is worth it. These tools will help you learn the rules.

Take this book as the first tool in your toolbox and refer to it often. Keep this book beside your bed, and make it your reference book long after you finish reading it. Use it as a tool and get a lovely journal for yourself and work between the two, dipping in and out as you need it.

Diary pages

—

At the end of each chapter, you will find some diary pages and some prompts to help you fill them in. There are many psychological benefits to writing things down, but one is that it helps you to 'think bigger'. This is precisely the aim of the game – and you are worth it. Let this little magic book become your private record. If you like, scribble your deepest desires and your darkest fears in the margins or in the pages provided at the end of each chapter. Underline the words or sentences that resonate with you. They will be safe in the privacy of these pages. Know and trust that your negativity and fears will start to dissipate almost immediately, while your positive thoughts, expectations and decisions will slowly increase and be made manifest in your reality. Come back to your diary pages six months from now and read again what you wrote. You will see how you have grown and what wonderful things you have created in your life.

DIARY PAGES

1 In the box, quickly sketch a child holding on to three kites. Your drawing represents you and your three desires.

2 Close your eyes and tune in to your three desires. Allow yourself to conjure up the feeling of these desires. For instance, feel the excitement growing in you at the thought of having a new car. In each kite write your desire.

3 Now if you wish, fill in your picture with other kites, as many as you like. Pick the desires that you have a deeper knowing about, or the one you feel is easier to imagine. Make these the closer kites. Put the desires that feel a lot more unobtainable further away.

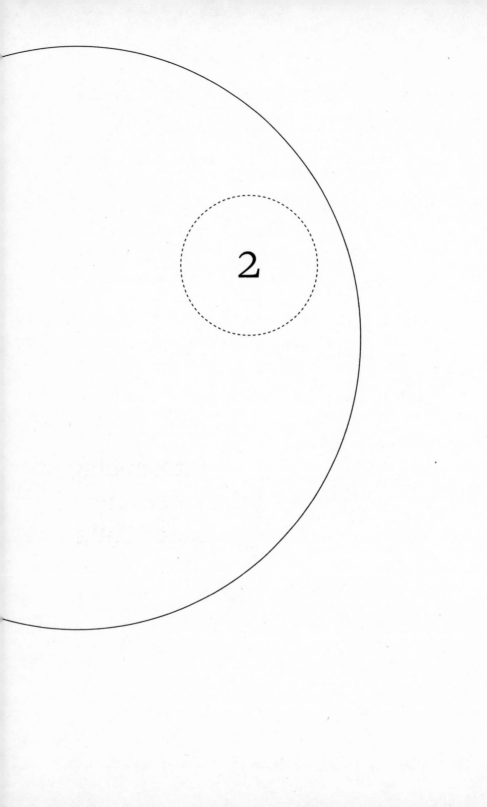

2

Introducing You to the Inner Child

IT IS TIME TO MEET YOUR INNER CHILD. The concept of your inner child is an important tool to represent and reprogramme your subconscious. Remember, the subconscious loves imagination and visualisation. When you build a relationship up with your inner child you can direct this child and tell it what to do. When you are feeling negative, this child needs your love and attention. If you can place your focus on this little child while staying in alignment with Source Energy, you have nearly all the ingredients you need to create what you want in your life. However, if you have ignored and abandoned your inner child you are limiting yourself greatly and your focus is compromised. It is really important that you know what this little child inside you is up to. Like all children, it has the potential to create great things or to create mayhem. If you can befriend your inner child you can use it as a tool to focus and master your mind.

I will help you coax this child to release the resistances blocking your way to bringing in what you are wishing for. This clever child has memorised every aspect and event of your life, both good and bad, and has stored them all in your subconscious. When your inner child is triggered, it can recall these aspects at will. The child then regurgitates these old events and relates them to what's happening in your present life. This is an automatic response. If you wish to change these responses you must get to know what your inner child is really doing. Your child is more than likely operating unsupervised and will block the way for you with fear of all kinds if you allow it.

Before we go any further with the process of how to deliberately create your own reality you must first bring your own inner little child with you on the journey. Hold her hand and away we go.

Here are some stories that will help you to see what I mean.

The story of the frightened little child
—

One day a little girl and her mother came to see me. The child had been through a very serious operation and it had been very painful for her. She was four years old and in those four short years she had been extremely ill. She had spent many nights of her life in hospital. She had been poked and prodded, injected and drugged. (Of course, this was all necessary and done in her best interests.)

When I saw her it was clear how traumatised she was. She was just out of hospital and would not leave her mother's arms. Terrified, she clung to her mother, viciously squealing at me if I even looked at her. She was like a wounded animal that would attack and bite you if you tried to attend to its wounds. This little girl would need careful nurturing.

Her subconscious had downloaded and filed everything that had happened to her. She now had many triggers that would send her into fear at the drop of a hat. As she grows up she may forget most of the details of her hospital experiences, but her subconscious mind will have recorded everything. Unless she receives the correct support she will no doubt carry these fearful feelings into her adult life. This will have a knock-on effect in a myriad of different ways. These fears act as a resistance and will block her from creating the life she wants for herself.

Your subconscious contains everything that has happened to you in your life. It is limitless. It stores all your experiences, good and bad. This influences how you go through life. Any negative experiences that have not been addressed are stockpiled in your subconscious and still beg to be acknowledged. You are walking around with a fearful little inner child leading the way. Unbeknownst to you, you are constantly affected and, to some degree, controlled by this child. When your subconscious is triggered it is like having a three-year-old take over your adult body. This is not maturity or adulthood. Real maturity requires you to love, nurture and take responsibility for this little one.

One of the most important relationships you will ever have is with your inner child.

There is a wounded child in us all. This hurt, bruised child is capable of attacking when triggered. When I see anger, or any other negative behaviour, in myself or others I always think this is the wounded inner child. This inner child is doing its best to protect itself. It is a child whose pain has not been acknowledged. Your inner child follows you around internally all your life, clinging to you, and this little one is afraid of any number of things that you may not even consciously remember. The little inner child blocks the way for your desires. She erects internal walls for protection.

Unfortunately these walls only keep others out. She may be trapped, inwardly frozen with fear. The child builds these walls for protection. The situation is long since gone but the feeling remains, and this acts as a barrier, a resistance holding you back from what you desire in life. Remember, your desires are like the strings of all your kites. These strings are in your hand and it is up to you to pull them to you. Sometimes you prevent your desires being actualised because of resistance. Resistance is a common denominator for us all and it comes through all negative feelings. For simplicity I will call it fear.

Imagine you are out having coffee with a friend. You bring your own child or a niece or nephew with you. The child plays with the other children while you have coffee. You are looking forward to having your chat with your friend. But something upsets the child and he is afraid. He comes over to you, tugging at your trousers. You ignore him and continue to chat. He tugs a little more and you tell him to go and play without paying much attention to his needs. But that's not going to cut it. The child's fears are gathering momentum. The little boy feels ignored, not seen and his fears have not been acknowledged. He is beginning to get more vocal.

You try to pacify him by giving him a snack. He flings it on the floor. Finally you stop chatting with your friend. You are frustrated and angry and so is he. You have not acknowledged him or his fear. By now the child's upset has gained momentum and he has added anger to the mix.

This is what your own inner child does to you every day. Any negativity you feel is your inner child trying to communicate with you. This negativity represents your fears and the child screaming. The child, metaphorically speaking, is tugging on your trousers trying to tell you there is something wrong with you. Unfortunately, you don't want to listen and you abandon, ignore and hide this child. Much as you would like your inner child to disappear, it won't. The only way to stop your inner child screaming is to acknowledge it and work with it to bring it, step by step, to a better place. Here is a little example from my own life.

'It is really important that you know what this little child inside
you is up to. Like all children, it has the potential to create
great things or to create mayhem'

JUDITH

A couple of years ago I recognised just how wounded my little child was, and decided to mindfully take responsibility for her. I was asked to work with a large group of executives, top professionals in their field. They were also an extremely stressed group of individuals who were daily faced with many difficult challenges and targets. I was delighted to work with them. But almost immediately after getting the contract I went into extreme fear. First, I acknowledged my inner child. I sat with myself to examine what this had brought up for me. I had worked many times with groups of people without this reaction. I knew I could not fulfil the contract with these people unless I was standing in my full personal power. In order to be effective I had to be aligned with Source Energy, not with fear. I knew I would only create momentum based on fear and the results of this type of creating would be limited. I wanted this to be a success for myself and for all the people who would be listening to me. So before developing my content for the seminar, my first point of contact was with my own inner little girl who was throwing a tantrum. I sat in meditation and I asked my little child for clarity on how to release this fear and resistance inside me.

During the days that followed I listened intently to my inner dialogue and noticed that I was repeatedly saying to myself one word – 'ridicule'. 'Ridicule, ridicule, ridicule' went over and over in my head. So I asked that reservoir of infinite intelligence inside me why I was afraid of ridicule. The answer came during a meditation. I got a sudden memory of when I was ten years old in primary school. When I was little I was extremely shy. Each day in school the teacher would make me stand up in front of everyone and ask me questions on what she had taught. For a painfully introverted child this was worse than pulling out every hair in my head. I remember wanting to disappear into the ground. This went on day after day for two years. As the teacher persisted I retreated further and further into myself. She was aggressive in her manner and that only compounded the problem.

Looking back on it now, she was probably trying to draw me out. But unfortunately it had quite the opposite effect. Despite a comforting family environment to go home to, in school I felt ridiculed in front of all the other children in the class. I had just found the answer to my current conundrum. The explanation for my present fear was deeply lodged in the psyche of my ten-year-old child.

My inner child had never been acknowledged and now she was tugging on my skirt until finally her internal screams, and my external fear, was loud enough that I couldn't ignore her any more. She was fed up with being neglected. I had a big problem. I needed to heal my little one quickly. For maximum effect and for the best outcome I had to present this seminar aligned with my adult self. There is no need for me to elaborate on the result of letting a ten-year-old child conduct proceedings. My inner child really believed she was stupid and feared being ridiculed. This is the record my subconscious was playing over and over. So I sat in a meditative visualisation with my hand on my heart and I started to connect with and comfort this beautiful, shy, innocent child. I gently spoke to her, telling her that she wasn't stupid at all, but she was traumatised by this experience and wasn't able to answer the teacher out of deep fear. I fully acknowledged the trauma for the first time in all those years.

As I sat quietly in a semi-meditative state I began to visualise going back in time. I saw my adult self standing beside my ten-year-old self in the classroom. I could visualise where I used to sit and the layout of the room. I could picture the teacher in my mind and although it was over 38 years ago it was vivid. It was like yesterday. In my mind's eye I spoke to my ten-year-old self. I explained that I was there now with her, whispering 'I have your back. I am your guardian and I am looking after you now.' I told her not to be afraid, that no one was allowed to ridicule her ever again. I told her I loved her and I was minding her. I was protecting her by my presence. I sat in meditation with my inner child every day for two whole weeks. I used every tool in my toolbox to keep myself aligned as I rewound the years. It was very difficult as it brought up a lot of pain around feeling stupid and inferior, not to mention profound feelings of fear. These were things that I had buried deep in my subconscious. I hadn't fully realised how they were affecting me in my life and now I was reprogramming myself.

At times during those two weeks I felt like jumping out of my own skin and running away. I also felt like cancelling the seminar, so that I wouldn't have to go through such uncomfortable feelings. This was big resistance. It was very tempting to abandon my inner wounded child. I didn't like feeling this way – it reminded me of how I used to feel. Obviously, how I used to feel was still how I actually was feeling, and the seminar had triggered it. But I had decided that I wanted to move forward in my life. Doing this seminar meant growth, both personal growth and the growth of my business. So I kept stepping through each feeling. I found placing my hand on my heart was a great tool in connecting me with my wounded child and I persisted in comforting her, instead of letting her go into a rant of fearful thoughts in my head.

On my last visit to the imaginary classroom, where my inner child was frozen in time and held rigidly in fear, I asked my little one to sing a song. She was obviously horrified. I encouraged her and asked her to trust in me. I would not let anyone harm her. I was undoing what was done. I was promising her it was safe for her to express herself. It is only by doing this kind of self-nurturing that you can heal the past. My little girl bravely started to sing and I visualised all the other little children singing too. My adult self laughed as I knew then that I had healed this deep-rooted fear of ridicule. Using alignment with Source Energy and my memories, imagination, visualisation, meditation and repetition, I was able to undo profoundly negative feelings stored in my subconscious mind. I replaced these negative feelings with a sense of security, trust and the feeling that it was safe to express myself without fear of ridicule.

I had met and acknowledged my fear and had re-parented my child. I was beginning to identify the fears of this inner child of mine and in doing so, recreating something different in awareness. This became exciting as I realised I could release my inner child and allow her to be who she really was, not what she had been moulded and conditioned to be. I was empowered. I took responsibility for her and decided to allow her to be free. I was not a tiny child feeling ridiculed. This was not my sum total. I had acknowledged, supported and empowered her. In doing so, I had created something entirely different internally in my life. The work was done and now it just had to ripple out into my external world.

I took my ten-year-old child with me the day I did the seminar. She was tucked under my wing. She felt safe and loved. She didn't feel the need to conduct the seminar through fear – her fear was gone. She was content and calm. I had aligned myself with Source Energy and proceeded from there. In releasing this 38-year-old block I released far more than ridicule. I didn't really understand just how much this particular issue had been affecting my life. The day I let go of this huge block in my life was the day a lot of my wonderful desires started to move toward me. My kites started to land, one after the other, and new kites started to appear on the horizon. This release was so powerful and the results were profound.

From that day on I became a wise mentor to my inner child. Every time I feel resistance within me I know it is her calling me. Her fear is a block for my kites or desires to come in. That resistance is what blocks me from deliberately creating my own reality. So I go to her and I put my hand on my heart and I talk to her. I then begin to comfort her until I bring her into alignment with that magnificent Source Energy inside me.

'I am gentle, kind and comforting to my inner child, as we uncover and release the old, negative messages within us.'

LOUISE L. HAYE

Your imagination and feelings are very important when dealing with your subconscious mind. Your subconscious cannot tell the difference between visualisation and reality. If you feel the visualisation is real then it is real to the subconscious. The subconscious feels. I conjured up the feeling inside me of being in that classroom. Therefore my subconscious mind really believed I was there. I also conjured up the feeling of strength and personal inner power, much as a strong parent would protect and mind a small child. I practised feeling this through my visualisation and reprogrammed the inner child with new thoughts. I repeated this over a period of two weeks to solidify it. By reprogramming I created a different response; this was a response I chose to create. It was an empowering response.

One of the most important healing tools you have in your toolbox is your relationship with your inner child. At the beginning you may not be able to visualise anything much at all. This is why having a picture of you when you were small is useful. Sometimes it helps to look at a child you love and recognise that you were once like that. Treat your own inner child as you would treat any child you love. Build this relationship up bit by bit and don't worry if you feel awkward at first. You can't get it wrong. It takes an average of 66 days to reprogramme your subconscious mind[1]. Using your inner child as a tool makes this much easier to achieve.

Key things to remember about your subconscious mind:

O Your inner child is a complete representation of your subconscious mind and all its aspects.

O Using the tool of the inner child gives you easy access to your subconscious mind.

O Your subconscious loves imagination, visualisation, loops, repetition and it reacts to feelings.

O It holds all memories both positive and negative and it can be triggered.

O When aligned with Source Energy it is infinitely intelligent.

O A few seconds of positive or negative internal chatter starts to program your subconscious, and it takes an average of 66 days to reprogramme it.

---

[1] Lally, P., van Jaarsveld, C. H. M., Potts, H. W. W., & Wardle, J. (2010). How are habits formed: Modelling habit formation in the real world. *European Journal of Social Psychology*, 40(6), 998–1009

DIARY PAGES

1 Get a picture of yourself as a child. Sit and look at it and write down what you see. Do you see a happy child, a sad or frightened child?

_____

_____

_____

_____

_____

_____

_____

_____

2 Write down what you would like to say to that child in the picture.

_____

_____

_____

_____

_____

_____

_____

_____

_____

3 Now, promise the child in the picture that you are going to look after and love her or him. Write your promise down.

....

....

....

....

....

....

....

....

4 Cast your mind to your three desires and tell your inner child that these desires are possible. You might not know how to manifest them yet, but they are possible.

....

....

....

....

....

....

....

PART TWO

The Seven Principles

1

Connect to Source Energy

'In life, if you can be still long enough to connect yourself to "The Source" – I call it God, you can call it whatever you like, Allah, the force, nature, the power – and allow the energy that is your personality, your life force to be connected to the greater force ... anything is possible for you. I am proof of that.'

OPRAH WINFREY

Tuning in

THE CROWN CHAKRA

Take a few moments to connect with yourself. Are you comfortable? Make sure you are cosy; maybe get a blanket and put it over your shoulders. If you like, loosen your clothes, take off your shoes and start to feel at ease. Bring your attention to your body. Relax your shoulders and slowly release the tension in your jaw and between your eyes at your brow. Gently place soft focus on your crown chakra at the top of your head. This chakra is your bridge to Source Energy. Close your eyes and while your focus is on your crown chakra, visualise the colour white or clear bright light. Now listen to the ebb and flow of your beautiful breath, ebbing and flowing, ebbing and flowing, ebbing and flowing ...

What you will learn from this chapter

—

By placing a soft focus on what to expect in this chapter you are positively influencing your subconscious mind. This will help you to receive the information in these pages. I will explain what Source Energy is, and who you are in relation to this energy. I will be giving you the main key to create with this infinite intelligence. You will begin to sense and explore your personal purpose for this lifetime, tune into your higher purpose and tentatively begin to create your own reality. This is what I call the Mysticism of Co-creation, or in other words, becoming aligned and creating with Source Energy. This is your spiritual dimension, the aspect of you that craves meaning, fulfilment and purpose in life.

Then, as with every chapter, I will share stories from my life, and the lives of Andrew and Kellie, to take you further into your journey. This will be followed with tools for your toolbox, which will be extremely helpful for creating your own reality in awareness. There will also be a powerful meditation specially designed to connect you with Source Energy, so please try to do it. It will help you look inward and step into your own inner light. My aim is to speed things up for you, so practising and participating in the exercises will bring you more quickly into the creative process. The diary pages are for your personal notes with a few little questions to ponder on if you wish.

What is Source Energy and what does it mean?

—

God, spirit, conscious awareness; people have used many different names over the centuries to describe what is essentially a mystery. Because many of these terms are loaded with negative connotations, I will refer to this infinite intelligence as Source Energy. This term avoids the traditional image of a patriarchal god. Source Energy transcends religion, domination, control, limitations and fear. It also opens the door for women to embrace this infinite intelligence from their own female perspective. Through generations, women and men have been subliminally conditioned to think of this vast, powerful energy as male. In fact, Source Energy dwells within us all equally. It is way beyond gender. This energy is imprinted on everything in the universe. Source Energy is not only the soul of the world, *anima mundi*, it is the soul of the universe. Source Energy expresses itself through the universe. The universe is the stage on which infinite intelligence acts out its compulsion to create. Source Energy is the director, and we are both the co-creators and the audience bearing witness to its marvellous performance.

Who are you in relation to Source Energy?
—

Every thought, idea or desire starts out as a spark of energy. The one-mind of Source Energy is unbounded consciousness. Consider this mind of Source Energy like a field of pure potential, or in other words, a place where everything is possible. All your ideas come from this field, and Source Energy seeks to express itself through you. It wants to use your talents and gifts to be seen in this world. Long before you were conceived in your mother's womb, you were conceived within the one-mind of Source Energy. I know this can be a bit 'heady', but it is really important for you to grasp who you really are and how wonderful you are. You are an extension of Source Energy, and therefore you are also pure potential. When you tune yourself into Source Energy, everything is possible – and I mean everything.

You came into this world, metaphorically speaking, as the energetic offspring of Source Energy. You are imbued with the ability to create limitlessly. What's more, the universe is your playing field. In effect you are made in the image and likeness of Source Energy. Where have you heard that before? All you have to do is acknowledge that this is who you are. Your crown chakra, when opened, will give you access to this higher consciousness and the best tool you have to do this is meditation and stilling the mind. As human beings we are all encoded with the capacity to express ourselves in different ways through our own natural talents. Acknowledging and embracing this energy in your life allows Source Energy to work in you and through you; it is utterly transforming.

We are all forged together, an infinitely intelligent integrated mass of energetic frequency, intermingling with each other, all connected and drawing from the same source. We are unconditional love, powerful, strong, limitless and abundant in health, wealth, joy and happiness. This is who you really are. If this is not how you feel, just for now, keep stepping, keep inching forward, one little bit at a time. There is great potential inside you – it just needs to be released.

Choice

—

Of course you can choose not to embody this energy. It is entirely up to you. However, if you do not acknowledge the power that lies within you, your creations will be limited. You will be relying on an egotistical

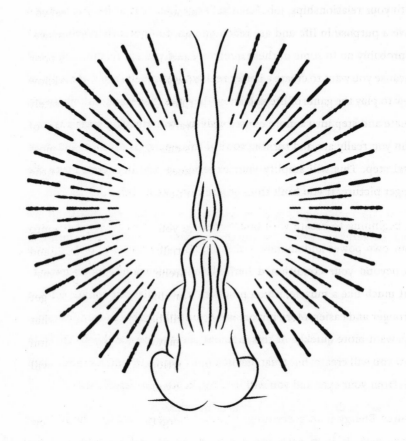

'Every thought, idea or desire starts out as a spark of energy.
The one-mind of Source Energy is unbounded consciousness.
Consider the one-mind of Source Energy like a field of pure
potential – a place where everything is possible.'

power based on fear, and not the limitlessness that emanates from Source Energy. You are cutting yourself off from the mains power supply and it makes no sense. Think about your life as it is now – are you happy with your relationships, job, financial situation, health? Do you feel you have a purpose in life and are reaching your full potential? The answer is probably no to some of these questions and you are reading this book because you want to create a better reality for yourself. You want to know how to play the game of life and know the rules. You want to deliberately create and step into a more consciously aware state. Becoming aware of who you really are and turning toward this energy is the first and most vital step. This will amplify your experiences and open you up to the bigger picture. If you can't think it you can't create it.

In beginning to create with Source Energy you start to step fully into your own power and abundant abilities. Initially, this will test you and go beyond your conditioned limited comprehension. This is normal. But much like a muscle, if you practise, your abilities to create will get stronger and easier. More importantly, you will be able to manifest what you want more quickly. At this moment you may not be able to envision how you will create, but trust me: in a short period of time the scales will fall from your eyes and you will be amazed at your own abilities.

Source Energy is in everything. It is our energetic breath, the Hebrew word *ruah*. It is in each and every one of us and everything in the universe. It has to be present otherwise you simply would not exist. I believe that once you exist you will always exist because Source Energy never dies. At our death our physical body may die, but that energy within us never dies.

Your intuition is the language of Source Energy whispering softly to you all the time, if you would only listen.

The key to deliberately creating your own reality with Source Energy

—

O The key to deliberate creation is to acknowledge who you really are. If you think limited, you are limited.

O You are an embodiment of Source Energy and by association you are unconditional love, powerful, strong, limitless and abundant.

O When you acknowledge that inner light of Source Energy you will start to create in awareness.

O Stop looking outside yourself.

O Opening your crown chakra will give you access to this powerful energy.

Remember, when you throw a pebble into water, it causes ripples. The ripples move from the inside out, never from the outside in.

Returning home and acknowledging Source Energy within you unites the divine and human parts of you. You merge with Source Energy. You become a deliberate co-creator. When you fully acknowledge Source Energy, and live it, it changes everything.

How do we feel emotionally and physically when we are connected to Source Energy?

O We feel inwardly powerful and strong.

O There is no fear, only unconditional love.

- We feel sure and definite.

- We feel loved and nurtured, whole, complete.

- We feel playful, happy and full of joy.

- We see the world from a broader perspective. I call this 'standing on the balcony'.

- We feel energetic and vital. We feel strong and solid.

- We look and feel lighter. We are vibrant beings and shine brightly.

How does this connection to Source Energy affect our personal lives?

- This rippling energy starts off deeply within our being, gradually starting to ripple out, becoming more visible.

- We begin to step into our personal purpose.

- We start to create positive momentum, generating abundance.

- This abundance comes in all sorts of forms, depending on our desires.

How does it affect society, humanity and the earth?

- Source Energy continues to ripple from you. These ripples get wider and wider.

- When you start to fulfil your personal purpose in life, then you begin to help others do the same – your family, children and friends benefit.

- You affect your lineage; generations of your ancestral line will benefit from you being the best version of yourself.

- One person deliberately creating is far more powerful than hundreds creating in unawareness.

- The universe works collectively and that includes you.

You then start to explore your higher purpose in this life. Awareness of the Mysticism of Co-creativity means that you are profoundly aware of the duty you have to your own life, and as a result you become aware of your profound duty to all of creation. When you step into your personal purpose you are ready to step into your higher purpose.

You are formed from energy – Source Energy. As a direct result of this union with Source Energy you are infinitely intelligent. Everything begins and ends with this pure conscious awareness.

Our mystical personal connection
—

The collective consciousness of Ireland has always been steeped in spirituality. The wonderful sacred sites that grace our landscape are proof of that. The Hill of Tara, Newgrange and Glendalough all bear testament to people tuning into Source Energy throughout the ages. It is precisely this connection to this infinite intelligence that leads us forward as a nation. Mary Robinson was right – she opened the way, as a woman, for people on the margins. But it is the people of Ireland, collectively, who have to align themselves with the calling of their soul. From female presidents to same-sex marriage, they are at the leading edge each and every day.

Now let's have a look at how Andrew, Kellie and I have embodied and integrated Source Energy into our daily lives and our mystical personal connection and experiences with Source Energy.

JUDITH

For me to be able to come to my creative ability in full I had to figure out the struggle that took place within me. I knew what Source Energy was to me internally and my relationship with it. But as a woman the conflict was my own personal mystical experiences versus what society and the Church told me about God and who I was supposed to be. The two didn't align.

I was always preoccupied with Source Energy. It's no wonder, really. I was born in 1968, when, for the most part, Ireland was in poverty and suppressed. The Catholic Church had a major influence in the lives of its people, including me. After Vatican II in 1965 there was a big shift in the Church. They were changing their image, moving away from the fearful image of God and toward the virtues of faith, hope and charity. This was the bind I was caught in. I was growing up standing on the bridge between two worlds, between two gods – the tyrannical God and the God of hope. Subliminally, as children do, I was absorbing everything and filing it deep in my subconscious mind. What I was amassing and storing had yet to make manifest in my reality and it most certainly would years later.

I have a vivid memory of being four years old and in my grandparents' house. My grandfather was dying upstairs in his bedroom and my grandmother and mother were nursing him gently as he laboured toward his journey's end. I remember praying on my knees in front of a statue of Mary, begging God not to let my grandfather die. Of course he died, or at least his physical body did. But his spirit remained with me until I was 26 years old. During this period I realised that we can never really die.

My fascination with Source Energy continued throughout my childhood. When I was six years old, just before I made my communion, I cornered a teacher in school, wanting to know explicitly what the Hail Mary actually meant. Not surprisingly, she couldn't give me a satisfactory explanation. However, I was extremely interested in Mary because she was female. For the large part, it didn't really bother me because I had my spirit grandfather and my God. In my childish mind I didn't really need any more saints or holy people. I already felt I had a direct line. Looking back, there was nothing childish in being fully tuned in to Source Energy, but I was totally oblivious to that; I just took it for granted.

All I knew as a child was that my God, the one that resided deep within me, wasn't scary. My God was there for me. My connection with my personal internal God was fully intact. When I wanted anything, I just went internally to this presence and I worked from there. I went straight to the top because I thought I could. In effect, my connection with Source Energy was completely open. I had no preconceived ideas of worthiness or unworthiness. I hadn't yet been conditioned by society to think I was full of sin. This was yet to come. I was just a child who loved her connection to Source Energy and used it all the time.

As I grew up I began to feel restricted by being female. My personal connection with Source Energy was strong, yet I was being ruled by a male-dominant society. I vividly remember feeling empowered as I watched female civil rights activists on the TV during the conflict in Northern Ireland. It was around 1976, when I was about eight years old. These women were always on the telly standing up for what they believed in. This took great personal courage, being women in a predominantly male environment. It was their courage that touched me. As a little girl, I was removed from the politics of it all, and just saw these young women amid a sea of men, standing in their own power.

I was beginning to realise that although I felt equal within my being, in the eyes of the world I wasn't equal. I was female and by virtue of my gender I was a second-class citizen. I was starting to see how conditioned and damaged society was, following generations of patriarchal dominance. I didn't like it one bit. It seemed to me, as a young girl, that the whole world was struggling for equality, and I was now experiencing it in my daily life. I listened to it on the radio, in school and on the TV.

Gradually, through all the Church controversies and hypocrisies I began to think 'Well, if this is God I don't want to know.' But my connection with Source Energy was still burning inside me. By now I was searching for answers.

Skipping ahead a few decades, I found myself among the first generation of Irish people to get divorced. My quest for spiritual answers also found me entering the cloisters of patriarchal power. It seemed so contradictory – given the Catholic churches views on divorce, I felt a bit like Mary Magdalene. I decided to do an honours degree in theology. By now I felt I was coming to God as a sinner. Personally I felt alienated and on the margins of Christianity. I didn't mind looking at it from the outside, though. I knew what God was to me internally. I never had any doubt about that. But the conflict within me was how to marry this internal God with the external, traditional image of God and generations of conditioning. I had a deep and compelling desire to understand and go beyond my conditioning.

In actual fact, I was welcomed to theology with open arms, and it was within the womb of the patriarchy I met and fell in love with Sophia for the first time. Sophia is wisdom, and thought to be the female representation of God in the Bible. This was the God of my childhood, the God I had a direct line to. This was the nurturing God I ran to in times of need. In my studies we were encouraged to make a relationship with Jesus, but Jesus, to me, represented a male. My struggle to be treated equally had meant asserting myself in my relationships with men. Expecting to be treated equally has often challenged and triggered generations of conditioning in the men around me, and they too often have an outdated image of how women in society should act. So I kept away from the image of Jesus, instead relating wholly to God. It was only through my studies, and when I was well into my forties, that I realised that the person of Jesus was an egalitarian. I had been brought up as a Catholic, I had gone to a school run by nuns, and it was only now that I was being told that Jesus was an egalitarian. I felt this information had been seriously and conveniently overlooked through the centuries.

I came to my studies as a seeker of truth. Working with Source Energy in my practice every day of my life left me in no doubt about its power and that it waits to be acknowledged in each and every one of us. During my studies I began to see how centuries of dominance disempowered both sexes. Not only women suffer; so do men. There is no balance. Men are stereotyped. The masculine, defined through generations, is expected to be in control, aggressive, powerful and strong. This really isn't fair on men, and it causes a lot of men serious anguish.

Sophia is the balance, the yin and yang. I could now reconcile the conflict within me. Throughout my life I had been conditioned by the male version of God, and that conditioning had affected every fibre of my life. It affects the lives of all women and men even without them realising it. Through going back into the cloisters of power I found the female version of God. Then, as a woman, I felt vindicated. But it doesn't stop at Sophia. Equality means equality for women and men.

Sophia was the missing piece, the female piece in the God puzzle. Once that piece is put into place it leads to a transcendence of all images of God. When the two pieces of the puzzle were put together it unveiled a genderless, raceless, colourless, powerful energy. Ironically, this was the same Source Energy that had been dwelling inside me all my life.

Yin and yang is a concept in Chinese philosophy that maintains that all things exist inseparably. Things that might appear opposites are actually interconnected. The interdependence and interrelationship between the female and male is an excellent example. They complement each other perfectly. They have to – they are a representation of the one body of Source Energy.

Acknowledging that Source Energy is who you are is fundamental in creating your own reality. You are a creator with this energy; you are only subservient to it if you are unaware of your relationship with it. This doesn't depend on any religion or sexual orientation. When you fulfil your personal purpose in life, your higher purpose starts to unfold.

I have always valued my right to vote. Each time I vote I remember all the wonderful women who fought for me to have that vote. I was 22 years old when Mary Robinson was elected President of Ireland and I remember crying when she made her inaugural speech, 'Mná na hÉireann agus fir na hÉireann ...' It still provokes the same reaction in me now. She went on to say, 'the Ireland I will be representing is a New Ireland, open, tolerant, inclusive'. For such a small island we pack a mighty punch when we want to. Andrew's story of the marriage equality referendum is testament to that.

ANDREW

For Andrew to come to his creative ability in the full he had to acknowledge the well of unconditional love that was within himself. As he says himself, 'You can do anything once you set your heart to it,' and this is always done in alignment with Source Energy.

The marriage equality referendum in May 2015 changed the Constitution of Ireland and extended civil marriage rights to same-sex couples. Throughout the campaign Andrew drew deeply from the well of Source Energy inside him. He mindfully paved the way for himself using this energy. I had the privilege of helping him to open up to, understand, hold and use this energy. Now I am paving the way for you to do the same.

In our sessions Andrew grew to mindfully apply himself to the principles of deliberately creating his own reality. He demonstrated how one person deliberately creating is far more powerful than hundreds creating in unawareness. To use the old idiom, Andrew and his colleagues were energetically singing from the one hymn sheet. We are all formed within the one-mind of Source Energy and we can connect with this energy individually or collectively. Andrew and his colleagues were collectively co-creating, and together they were adding fuel to this energetic fire.

During the campaign Andrew and his colleagues changed years of repression and abuse into liquid gold. Alchemy was taking place. Ireland was getting a chance to redeem itself and all its controversies through a collective consciousness. The eyes of the world were opened by Andrew and many others who did not surrender to the reality of the Church and State. Instead, they co-created their own reality based on equality and love.

His journey encompassed all the steps contained in these pages as he created his own reality. Andrew created in various degrees of awareness. As he stepped nearer and nearer to Source Energy he gained greater clarity and rapidly achieved results. The more he incorporated Source Energy, the more powerful and positive his creations became. He was innately guided every step of the way. He may not have fully recognised this guidance in the earlier stages, but by the time the vote was called he had no doubt about this powerful Source Energy within him.

Andrew recollects that his first encounter with Source Energy was in primary school. A priest was giving a blessing and laid his hands on Andrew's head. He remembers feeling a strong sense of unconditional love pass through him. Over the years Andrew tapped into Source Energy through yoga and meditation. (One of his greatest encounters with Source Energy, in Bali, left an indelible mark on him, and I will be elaborating on this in Chapter 2: Alignment.)

However, the term 'god' did not fully express what Andrew had experienced. This energy transcended the traditional concepts of the man-made god that he felt shunned him. This powerful Source Energy was fully accessible to Andrew, regardless of his sexual orientation. The traditional image of god has marginalised gay people, and for many people this image represents conditional love. Source Energy, however, goes way beyond this antiquated model, leading us into the hope of a brighter future with unconditional love as its foundation.

Source Energy had graced Andrew with the knowledge that unconditional love existed. This energy was priming him for what was to come. He had tuned into this energy and would draw upon it during fraught times in the campaign. This solidified his deep knowledge that this energy was vast and not limited to any particular sexual orientation or religion. He felt that he was an integral part of life and not separated because of his sexual identity. He realised that Source Energy resides in each and every one of us. Andrew had found his own personal treasure trove, with a limitless supply of unconditional love within him. Andrew mindfully accessed and deliberately used this treasure trove of abundant energy often during the campaign by aligning himself through meditation and using the steps and tools provided in this book. He had established his connection, embodied it and now he was ready to live it.

KELLIE

Kellie, for the most part, and much like most of us, had always taken for granted her connection with Source Energy, so much so that it was only after her accident, when she was shocked out of alignment, that she began to appreciate what she had naturally been doing. It was when she tuned out that she realised that she had been so tuned in. Her accident brought with it a realisation. Her journey back to alignment and her full creative ability was now being done in awareness.

Kellie had always accepted what was being given intuitively to her. She very seldom questioned it. She didn't resist it. While some of us can be busily looking outward for the answers, Kellie almost always stayed true to herself. Kellie recognised her inner light, holding to Source Energy deep inside, and the more attention she paid to this inner light flickering inside her the more it grew and developed. It became her norm. It was an automatic response for Kellie to go inwards to Source Energy for the answers. She naturally listened to her intuition, but Kellie simply didn't recognise that that was what she was doing. She knew she was doing something right but she didn't quite know what it was. Then the accident happened. What lay ahead for her, and her journey with me, has meant she has become more consciously aware of how she creates with Source Energy. This has enabled her to take the large leap from unawareness to awareness, becoming a very powerful deliberate creator.

Her adventures, much like Andrew's, incorporate all the principles in this book. In learning to use them, you too will take that leap in consciousness.

Kellie's awareness of the presence of Source Energy came through her intuition. Your gut instinct is the voice of Source Energy. The voice of Source Energy never stops calling you, but you have the freedom to listen to it or not. That internal voice will never abandon you, especially not in times of need. This was what Kellie was about to find out. Her skill in listening to her intuition was about to become the most important thing in her life. She was on the cusp of entering into a fearful period and in doing so ran the risk of shutting down her connection to Source Energy altogether.

After her accident she had been shocked out of her natural state, and now more than ever it was imperative that she regain her alignment with Source Energy. If she didn't, her fearful inner child would take over the steering wheel of her life and her adult self would merely be the back-seat driver.

Source Energy has a language all of its own. As you listen more, and tune in, you will learn how to decipher what it is saying to you. Your intuition is like your internal navigation system: when you listen to the directions you will get to your destination every time. When you go against it you will end up in the rough.

The little meditation below (also available on my website) will help you focus on the wonderful light that is inside you. It will encourage you to look to it, appreciate it and let it shine. It will help you to honour it by not letting anyone else try to blow it out. You will begin to learn to love it instead of trying to hide it. Once you have stepped into this inner light you will begin to fulfil your life's purpose and create with Source Energy. Then you will start to move towards your own higher purpose for your life and who knows where you will go from there.

MEDITATION – SEE THIS LIGHT OF MINE

Just for a few minutes, get nice and comfortable. Relax your body. Close your eyes and feel for any tension in your body. Gently decide to let it all go. You are at ease, listening to your breath ebbing and flowing, ebbing and flowing, ebbing and flowing …

Bring your attention to your feet, wiggle your toes and move your ankles in a circular motion. Slowly bring your awareness to your legs and let go of any pent-up energy in your muscles, thighs and hips. Breathe into your hips and release any tension that is preventing you moving forward.

Move your attention to your root chakra, the area at the base of your spine. It is a beautiful shade of red. Allow your perineum muscles to relax and feel negative energy flow out from you. The negative energy that is being released from you is drawn into Mother Earth and it naturally dissipates. Move your attention up to the area below your belly button. This is your sacral chakra, and it is a warm orange colour. Hold your focus there for a few seconds and breathe into this area; this is your creative chakra. With a big breath in and out, release any tension you are carrying in this area. Gradually move up to your solar plexus chakra above your belly button. This chakra is a soft yellow shade. Now focus your attention there, and breathe, releasing any bottled-up energy. Release all your tightly clenched stomach muscles.

As this energy continues to move up towards your heart chakra, you see a lovely green colour. Breathe love into to your heart and release any stresses. Breathe love in and breathe negativity out. Allow this energy to continue to your throat chakra. This chakra is a clear crisp blue. Open your mouth and breathe out any negativity. Breathe in joy, breathe out any resistance in you. Anything you have not been able to say, any blocks or any frustrations – just release them and let them go by breathing them out.

Bring your attention to your third eye chakra, your seat of intuition. Draw your focus in at the centre of your forehead and visualise the colour indigo. As you breathe in, imagine that you are sending your breath into this area. Now focus on your crown chakra, which is a gleaming electric white colour. Again, breathe and visualise your crown chakra opening slowly. As you allow this chakra to open, feel streams of clear positive conscious awareness fill this area.

Your whole body is now porous. Each time you breathe in and out you are breathing in and out from all your chakras. You are absorbing Source Energy through every orifice. Sit with this energy for a minute, just gently breathing from every cell, organ and gland in your body.

Now, softly bring your attention back to your heart chakra. Gently focus on this area and imagine a beautiful bright flickering light, like the light of a candle, filling your heart. Breathe deeply into your heart. As you do this the oxygen fuels the flame and it gets bigger and bigger, brighter and brighter. It is a beautiful soft golden glow and as you breathe you feed it and it expands. This is your inner light of Source Energy. Feel this wonderful radiant light flow into every cell in your body. See it in your mind's eye as it ripples out into your auric field, the energy field around you. As you breathe, you fuel this beautiful flame even further and it flows out to your family and friends. With each breath it spreads further and further out into your workplace and all the people you haven't physically met yet. On it goes, out into Mother Earth and further still into the entire universe. This energy that is emanating from you is Source Energy. It is powerful, strong, unconditional, limitless and abundant. This is who you really are.

Now breathe this universal energy back into your body. Bring your attention back to your own powerful beating heart. Put your hand on your heart and slowly bring your attention back in, and when you are ready, open your eyes.

TOOLBOX

Gentle meditation or visualisation (if you can't, don't worry for now)

Using your journal or the diary pages

Starting to observe and listen to your intuition a little bit more

Reiki for stress reduction

DIARY PAGES

1 Can you remember experiencing Source Energy as a child?

....

....

....

....

....

....

....

2 How do you experience Source Energy in your life now?

....

....

....

....

....

....

....

....

....

3 Do you listen to your intuition, which is the voice of Source Energy?

....

....

....

....

....

....

....

4 Imagine the field of pure potential. Now draw a quick sketch of your three desires in the field of pure potential, just waiting for you.

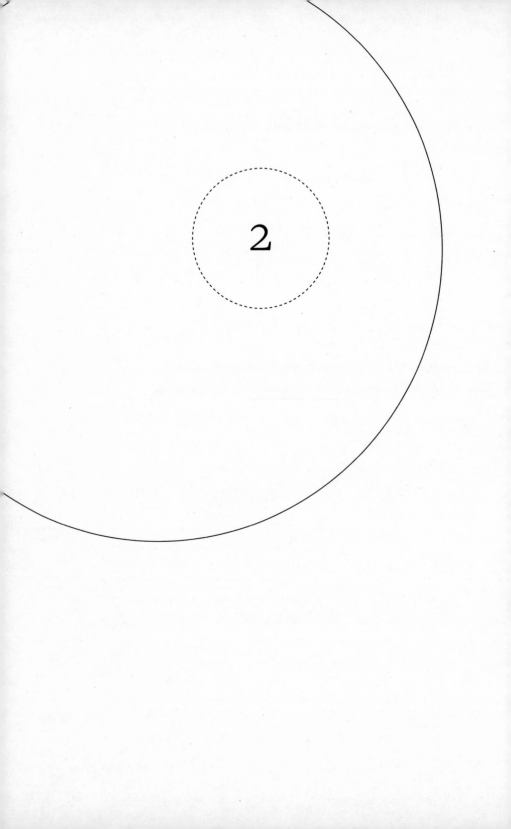

2

Alignment

'When your consciousness is directed
outward, mind and world arise. When it is
directed inward, it realises its own Source
and returns home into the unmanifested.'

ECKHART TOLLE

Tuning in

THE THIRD EYE CHAKRA

Remember this is your precious time for yourself. If you have

any incense, use it, or simply light a candle and watch it for

a moment. Make sure that you are comfortable. Gently relax

your jaw and ease the tension in your forehead. Allow yourself

to relax. Becoming easy with yourself enables you to tune in

to Source Energy and the field of pure potential. Bring your

attention to your third eye chakra, on your forehead between

your eyes. This is the seat of your intuition. If you have any

lavender oil, massage a small drop into this area. Now close

your eyes and place inward focus on your third eye chakra,

softly visualising the colour indigo. Listen to your beautiful

breath. Just like the tide, it is ebbing and flowing, ebbing and

flowing, ebbing and flowing ...

———

What you will learn from this chapter

—

The journey in this chapter will be toward aligning yourself with Source Energy, so I will be elaborating on what alignment actually is. Being aligned with Source Energy is vital to create the life you want to lead. Part of aligning with Source Energy is learning to tune your own mind in. Therefore throughout the chapter there will be plenty of imagination, visualisation and metaphors, all things that your subconscious mind loves. You will slowly start to become aligned naturally as you read. I will do the groundwork with you first and explain what triggers blocks to alignment, how you can tune yourself out, the negative signs to look out for, tuning in to other people instead of yourself, and what intuition is. Then we will be getting to work to align you. For maximum benefit I suggest that you take part in all the exercises.

There are certain aspects that you really need to know before you start deliberately creating. I will use the radio station as a metaphor to explain alignment and the way it works. I have also adapted the four stages of learning to incorporate Source Energy and alignment.

One of the keys to deliberately creating is aligning, looking after and nurturing your own inner child. I will be inviting you to work with your little one. Your inner child is of paramount importance, and I fully expect this little child to be acknowledged and nourished throughout these pages.

I will explain what causes blocks to creating your own reality; more important, I will give you tools to help release these blocks. I will give you an insight into why alignment is vital through examples from my own life and from the lives of Andrew and Kellie. From these examples you will see how we have moved into alignment and the effects this has had on our lives. You can do the same. The benefits of personal alignment are incredible. Personal alignment leads to fulfilling your personal purpose. In turn, this will lead to exploring your higher purpose in this lifetime.

I will give you plenty of tools for your toolbox, and your diary pages will be there for you to write and ponder on the questions asked.

What does alignment with Source Energy mean?

—

Being aligned with Source Energy is the first and most important step to creating the things you want in life, be that in love, your career, relationships, money or simply happiness and joy.

Your crown chakra is the doorway to Source Energy. Aligning yourself with this energy allows your third eye chakra to unfold. Alignment with Source Energy is the point where the divine and human meet within you.

O Alignment means being fully connected to infinite intelligence with no interruptions and no resistance, with full access to the field of pure potential and infinite creative abilities.

O It is listening to and clearly hearing your intuition, which is the voice of Source Energy.

O When you are fully aligned you tap into unconditional love, feel invigorated, joyful and happy.

O Mentally you are aligned with your subconscious and conscious mind.

O Physically your spine is aligned and your body is relaxed and healthy.

O Emotionally you are balanced and you are in the flow.

O Your chakras are balanced.

O Your intuition and psychic abilities are greatly heightened, as are your visualisation and imagination skills.

When you create your reality from a place of alignment you are at your most powerful. It is not ego-driven, it is always fuelled by love. Your ability to stay aligned depends on how much attention and how much importance you place on keeping yourself there. You can fluctuate in and out of alignment many times during the day, or you can practise keeping yourself in a more constant state of alignment. The results from a steady state of alignment are remarkable. You become a deliberate creator. Everything flourishes when you are in harmony with Source Energy, from health to wealth, joy and happiness.

You are in synchronicity with your life; it is, as Carl Jung puts it, 'a falling together in time, a kind of simultaneity'.

The radio station

—

Your subconscious loves imagination and visualisation, so let's speak to your subconscious mind in a way it will understand.

The metaphor of an old-fashioned radio might help you to solidify the concept of alignment. Imagine that to be tuned into Source Energy your radio dial should be set at 100FM. But you have been fiddling with the dial and you have tuned out. The station you are picking up is at 90FM. Slowly you begin to recognise that you would prefer a different station, one that is not so melodramatic and depressing. You don't know how to retune the radio, but there must be a better station somewhere, so you begin to turn the dial.

While you are trying to tune yourself in there might be some interference on the way, and you may pick up other stations. But you don't give up, and with a bit of perseverance, you fine tune until eventually you find 100FM. Once the station is set you are free to enjoy it. You are now consciously aware that you can tune yourself into the station you like.

In making your decision to tune into Source Energy, you are effectively tuning yourself in to a higher vibrational frequency, one that is more vibrant, abundant and uplifting.

What are the four stages of learning?

—

This will give you some idea of what stage you are at. Don't worry; with a bit of practice it will all come very quickly. It's a bit like going to the gym: you start out pretty unfit but it doesn't take long to build a bit of muscle and see results.

STAGE 1

O You don't realise you are the co-creator of your own reality.

O You don't know what alignment with Source Energy is.

O You think your life is not working out. This is due to outside forces and you have no control.

O In unawareness, you are creating from a negative mindset.

O These negative creations are based on outdated learned behavioural patterns and conditioning.

O Your life is reflecting your negative thoughts and you are creating a negative loop.

For example, picture this. As a child, your father was very controlling and dictatorial, and you were always nervous and fearful in his company. When addressed by him you would fumble and speak really quietly, which would only aggravate him more. These memories of a 'scary' authoritative figure are stored deep within your subconscious mind. However, you are unconsciously unaware of this.

Many years later you find you have a very dictatorial and controlling boss at work. Again, in unawareness, you are triggered by old memories of your 'scary' father, and every time your boss makes an appearance you react like a frightened five-year-old child. You are now creating from a negative memory and mindset. This begins to annoy your boss and you begin to create a negative loop, and there goes your promotion.

STAGE 2

O You don't know how to create your own reality.

O But you do want to learn.

O At a deep-rooted level you have made a decision that it is time for great change.

O But at the beginning it is hard to grasp this new awareness.

To continue the example: you begin to realise you are creating this negativity with your boss. You decide there has to be a better way. You realise that perhaps you need to work on yourself rather than blaming circumstances and creating more negativity. But you don't really know where to start. At this stage you are now consciously aware.

STAGE 3

O This is acknowledging the presence of Source Energy within you.

O Understanding that alignment is the inward juncture where the divine and human meet.

O You are knowingly tuning yourself in and applying and practising the processes.

O This will mean a reprogramming of old patterns.

O This is where a period of self-observation and conscious focus takes place.

O You have to ignore what you have already created in your life (sometimes that's very hard) and align your mind to new, more positive thoughts.

O By using all your tools you begin to deliberately create your own reality.

Going back to the example: you begin gradually to take the first steps. You observe your behaviour and start to align yourself by listening finally to your intuition telling you there is something wrong. You start to reprogramme yourself and the loop you have created from childhood with your authoritarian father. These are the first steps to creating a new reality for yourself and your boss. Now you are one or two steps closer to your promotion.

Remember, this ability has always existed within you. Source Energy has been waiting patiently for you to acknowledge it. You were always creating your own reality, but now you are beginning to do it positively and in awareness through alignment.

STAGE 4

O This is stepping positively into deliberately creating your own reality until it becomes second nature to you.

O You begin to do it automatically and the results are fantastic.

'Take the first step in faith, you don't have to see the whole staircase, just take the first step.' DR MARTIN LUTHER KING JR.

Finally, with a bit of practice, you start to erase your old fearful childhood memories and stand firmly in your adult self. You begin to get on with your boss, realising that his controlling ways are fears he has carried from his childhood. With this insight your internal negativity ceases and is replaced with more positive feelings. You have now changed your inner reality and that is being reflected in your relationship with your boss. You ultimately get your promotion.

It's a bit like riding a bike or driving a car: at first it seems difficult, but after a little practice you become great at it. Then it becomes an automatic response. There can be some difficult moments when you are trying to tune in, and in the early stages you will tune out more often than not. It will take a while before you are fully convinced of the benefits of alignment with Source Energy, and sometimes you might feel like giving up. It is much easier to go back to old familiar patterns. These patterns become a negative comfort zone for you. But just keep inching that dial closer. Use all your tools in your toolbox. This is a big decision to start looking for and tuning into Source Energy. It is a major shift in your evolution, and this may take time to integrate.

If you don't like your current reality, try to ignore it for the moment. This is what you have already created in unawareness. It's like yesterday's paper – old news. The outer manifestations are simply a result of what you have been creating internally. The internal negativity has been made manifest in hard matter. Changing your inner reality will reflect in your outer world. Work on the 'inner' and the 'outer' looks after itself.

Triggers, resistances and blocks to alignment

—

There are many degrees of alignment. It is possible to be fully aligned, partially aligned or not aligned, all in one day. Old negative experiences are pockets of fear becoming layered like an onion over the years. These fears profoundly and subliminally affect our lives. Your kites or desires get stuck and wedged firmly in the tree of procrastination, which prevents them coming in to land.

What does your subconscious do?

O It has stored all your memories, both positive and negative.

O If something negative is triggered within you, your subconscious will remind you.

O This reminder becomes the resistance to moving forward.

O Certain things will set you off.

O Procrastination is fear and it can take over.

These are blocks standing between you and your desires. In other words, your fears stand in your own way. You will draw from the well of past negative experiences that lie deep within. You will pull them out and conjure these feelings up at will without even knowing you are doing so. The constant negative chatter in your head gets louder and louder. This becomes habitual and, unfortunately, in doing this you will also be dragging yourself out of alignment, perhaps only momentarily, but it can also become the predominant way you live your life. You can easily tell if you are not aligned. Listen to your thoughts and words – this will give you a big clue to help you decipher whether you are in the negative or positive. Think of this scenario – you would like to lose weight and improve your health, but when you consider changing your eating habits you think of all the diets you have tried in the past and how you have failed to stick to them. The chatter in your head is telling you that you can't do it. This can have minor or major repercussions. But everything is creating something!

ANGER

Another block that comes between you and what you want to create in life is anger. Anger can become very easy to conjure up. It is possible to be very angry for much of your life. If you create predominately from anger you are not aligned with Source Energy. Therefore your ability to create will be limited. It is much like the volume on your radio. You can turn it up towards the positive or down towards the negative in varying degrees – it is up to you. But creating from anger blocks your positive flow. I will be dealing with how to release these blocks throughout each chapter.

Wheel of life

—

These are some signs of being tuned out from Source Energy.

O You may be suffering from anxiety, depression or fatigue.

O Your financial situation and bank balance will reflect your alignment.

O Your love life will reflect your alignment, whether positive or negative.

O Your job or business opportunities will give you signs of the state of your alignment.

O Are you happy? Is everything easy in your life? Is there joy?

Take a look at your life at the moment and see what areas seem to be in the negative. Opposite, you will see a wheel consisting of eight sections. Imagine these sections combined represent your life. This wheel of life is a tool in helping you to see what areas of your life you are more tuned in to and those areas you have tuned out from. Take a moment to rate your level of alignment in each of the eight areas with a dot. But remember to be honest with yourself while doing it. If you rate a zero, this means you are not satisfied or not aligned to this area of your life, while ten means you are extremely aligned and satisfied in this area. When you are finished, connect all the dots together. This will give you a clear idea of the areas in your life that are in the negative.

When you recognise that you are not aligned, it means that your little fearful inner child is calling. Observe yourself; listen to your internal chatter. Start to identify when you have tuned out. Don't worry if you're thinking, 'I don't think I have ever been tuned in.' Many of us spend much of our lives tuned out, or not even remotely on the same radio station as Source Energy. You can spend your entire life trying to create a positive reality from a negative stance. You are trying to grow roses but you are planting potatoes.

Getting to know your inner child and negative signs
—

Getting to know what's really going on in your own mind is extremely important so befriending your inner child is a great tool to get access to vital information.

'This wheel of life will help you see what areas
of your life you are tuned out from'

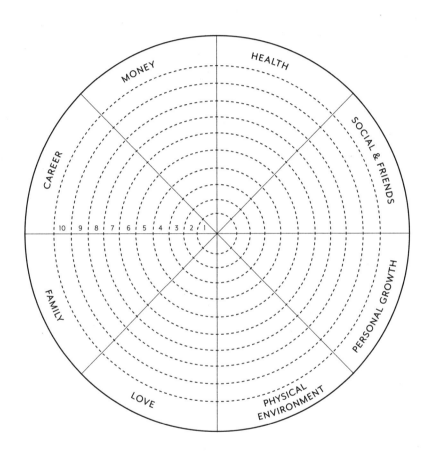

Do you remember the story of Little Red Riding Hood? She set off through the woods on the way to her grandmother's, and when she got lost she was very frightened. All she needed was to be gently guided back to the path, but she thought there was nobody there to help her and she felt alone. This simple fairy tale has powerful connotations and can reflect back to you what is happening in your own life. When you stray too far from being aligned with Source Energy you become very fearful and feel horribly alone.

Your inner child will give you clear signs when she is not happy, so tune in and start to listen. Here are a few examples:

O A negative internal dialogue perpetually playing over and over in your inner world,

O over-sensitivity,

O panic attacks,

O feeling your temperature rise, your pulse quicken or butterflies in your stomach,

O extreme anger,

O carrying a lot of tension in your body.

By listening to the doubts and fears of this little child and the way she expresses them (physically, mentally, emotionally), you get a feel for what you will eventually create in your external world. In times of crisis it can seem hard to imagine that Source Energy even exists, never mind aligning yourself with it and observing your inner child. However, it is precisely at this point when you need it most. Believe it or not, this is your quickest way out of your dilemma.

Tuning yourself in to another person's route

—

Becoming too fearful to listen to, let alone trust, your own inner guidance system is detrimental. It leads to trusting the internal navigation system of those around you. But be warned: following someone else's route can lead you to concentrate on their journey, not yours, and moving further away from your own alignment. Sometimes it is easier to 'do' for everyone else and not 'do' for yourself.

O You put everyone else first, with little or no regard for your own alignment. This is something many women are prone to doing.

O You are trying too hard to make something work, be it a career, relationship or a vocation.

O You are trying to hold everything together.

O You are trying to spare other people's feelings at the expense of your own.

O You are afraid of breaking with tradition.

O You fear committing some kind of 'sin' or are scared of becoming a social outcast.

O You are trying not to be selfish.

Whatever the reason, if you are not looking after yourself and your own alignment you are depriving yourself and others of the aligned, fantastic you. This is the version of you that is limitless, the real you that unconditional love creates in awareness and positivity. When you are not aligned you do more harm than good. Nobody gains from being unaligned; nobody is happy underneath it all. Remember the ripple effect – the ripples always move from the inside out, not the outside in. If you are rippling from the outside in, you are going against natural law.

Your intuition

—

O Make a clear distinction between your intuition and your negative internal dialogue. Your intuition, or gut instinct, is the soft voice of Source Energy inside you. When you are aligned your third eye chakra opens and your intuition starts to flow. It speaks to you in ideas, thoughts, memories, songs, nature, visualisation and imagination; someone will say something that will give you insights.

O Your intuition is always calling you. Stop running away from it. Turn towards it, and you will start to hear what it is saying to you. It is there somewhere and you will find it. I call it 'gnawing' when something is at you and you keep ignoring it or putting it last. Sometimes you start off on the right track listening to your intuition. But then you get side-tracked and veer away from it. Sometimes you don't want to listen to your intuition because you know full well what it is saying, and you are afraid of what you know you need to do.

This resistance to acknowledging and listening to your intuition is because it may mean great change and you are afraid of what that change will bring. You think that not listening to your deepest truth will save yourself and others from negativity. But really this denial of self will eventually catch up with you and in time create a bigger problem.

This is what I call 'doing an ostrich', keeping your head firmly stuck in the sand. It happens a lot and it can keep you stuck for years, if not a lifetime. Some people dig a big negative hole for themselves; then, when they get the intuition that it is negative, instead of getting out of the hole and covering it up, they keep digging and digging.

The more you ignore your intuition, the louder your inner child screams. Eventually you will have to listen as it will make itself manifest somewhere in your life at some level. When the problem is small you can minimise the damage by listening to your intuition. The consequence of not listening to this internal navigation system means that your inner child or fear is in control of your life. She isn't happy. She is revving up to have a tantrum because you are ignoring her. How tuned out you have become will be reflected in the amount of negativity you will create in your life. This all adds up. Source Energy has a language all of its own. When you are aligned you can hear and understand this language. Your intuition is the natural voice of Source Energy. If you do not listen to your intuition you will be led astray every time. When you are not aligned, your internal navigation system or intuition is always telling you to stop, divert and go back.

This brings me to how unique and special you really are, and the sooner you realise this the better.

You are special and uniquely aligned

—

It is the same Source Energy within you that is present in everyone and every living thing. But what distinguishes your energy from mine? It is the intrinsic way this energy works individually within and through us. Being aligned is the point where the divine and human meet, so, just as every snowflake is unique, the way this infinite intelligence expresses itself through you is uniquely yours. Source Energy conveys itself exclusively through your talents and gifts. It discloses itself individually through your physical appearance and the colour of your skin, your gender and sexual orientation. Source Energy reveals itself in the circumstances of your conception through the Mysticism of Co-creation. It is present in every aspect of your life.

You are a means for this magnificent energy to work for and through you. It is your choice to become aligned with this infinite intelligence or not. The alternative is to stay the way you are. There is no wrong or right. There is no judgement.

Remember, your subconscious loves imagination and visualisation, so please do this exercise with me as a means to access your subconscious mind and to start reprogramming it in alignment with Source Energy.

VISUALISATION: THE BUS OF LIFE

When you keep going further and further away from your own connection, you become lonely and unhappy. Unfulfilled and depressed, you may find yourself lacking on all levels, including financially. Your fearful little child is now in the driving seat of your life.

Just for a minute, visualise your own inner child behind the wheel of the bus of your life. This child is careering down the motorway, hitting all the cats' eyes, bump after bump after bump. She is out of control. Again and again, she swerves in the nick of time to avoid disaster after disaster. Then she heads for the hard shoulder and starts ploughing through the grass.

Now imagine sitting next to her in the driver's seat. Gently put your arm around her and comfort her. She is completely overwhelmed at being in the driving seat of your life and she is doing her best. As you hold her with one arm, lightly take the wheel with the other hand. Lovingly explain to her that you are in control now. At first she will be afraid to give you the wheel, but eventually she will be delighted to be free to play.

Start aligning yourself right now

—

The child driving is your deep-rooted fear. You are now going to gradually align this fear with who you really are – Source Energy. You are not the sum total of your fear. When you acknowledge and start to connect with your frightened inner child, you will get great results. You are beginning to comfort her and direct her. Decide right now to acknowledge your inner child's fears. This will enable you to bring her with you on your new journeys. Otherwise she will be hanging from you, screaming with frustration and blocking your every step.

Work with me right now. Put your hand on your heart and tell her you will never abandon her again. By putting your hand on your heart you are positively conditioning yourself to connect to the child immediately. Promise her that you are taking her home to that inner light. This is her exclusive intimate connection with Source Energy. You have begun to listen to your internal navigation system again and all is well. From now on I would like you to continuously comfort your fearful inner child. Please tell her she comes first from now on. Soothe her. She is a great little one.

How will you know when she is needy? You will know by observing your behaviour. When you are angry, fearful and upset, this is the child within you needing attention. You could be at work, out socially or at home. It doesn't matter. Observing the way you feel will give you a clear indication of whether or not the child needs you. When the child is negative, observe and acknowledge this by putting your hand on your heart and asking her why. Placing your hand on your heart is an easy and powerful tool in acknowledging and comforting your inner child. In the beginning you could end up doing this an awful lot.

Then listen. Listen to your intuition. Remember, your intuition is the voice of Source Energy. It will give you a clear indication of why that child is upset. You may get a negative memory. A word or a song might remind you of something you have long forgotten. Ask the child what is wrong and you will get the answer. Asking is vital. You cannot receive if you do not ask. The answers to your questions will be provided by that infinite intelligence within you. Just listen for the answers. They may not come straight away, so while you wait just comfort the child. This inner child has been ignored for a long time. You have been avoiding her. Or perhaps you are totally disconnected from her, so she feels abandoned and is blocking your way. You are taking complete responsibility for this child now, so you have to stop blaming anyone else for her behaviour. Explain to her that she is free to do whatever is her heart's desire. You will always have her back. Tell her you love her and will never leave her alone again.

Highlighting the dos and don'ts
—

I have selected the example below from my own life to underline a very important point: you cannot create your own reality consistently, positively and in awareness until you align yourself. It is impossible. So this example is all about me starting to move towards alignment and beginning to fulfil my own personal purpose in life. It is from a time when I had come very far away from my own inner child. It also highlights that no matter how far removed you are from being tuned in, Source Energy is waiting patiently for you.

This period of ignoring my own alignment led to huge resistance in my life. As I made my way back to the infinite intelligence I needed to support myself, I used all my tools in my toolbox and acquired some more. Meditation is the most effective tool, but at that stage I found it difficult to meditate. I was too anxious. I was looking outward to such a degree I couldn't even give my little inner child any nurturing. I had to slowly bring myself into alignment. The thought of quietening my mind to sit in meditation seemed impossible. Paradoxically, I thought I didn't have time to meditate, but the truth was that I didn't have time not to. But I had to step gently to this realisation – and that's okay. Looking back, I realise that I could have sped up the process no end had I meditated. I was caught in a loop. So I used the tools I felt more comfortable with, the tools I found more manageable at the time.

JUDITH

As a child I was, like most children, extremely aligned to Source Energy. I took this connection for granted. It was probably during my early thirties that I gradually and without realising it moved slowly but surely away from my centre. Due to a combination of events over a period of time my confidence had diminished. I was now married. I had twin boys and a beautiful daughter. There were many wonderful aspects to my life. Nonetheless I began to completely forget about my connection with Source Energy.

I moved further and further from my own alignment with this powerful energy within me. In doing this, I had seriously abandoned my inner child. I didn't put my own needs first or even put them into the equation. I had allowed myself to be conditioned by society, to fill the societal expectations of a married Irish Catholic woman with children. I was creating the same negative patterns as millions of women and men throughout millennia. Those same patterns that I had seen others falling into, I now fell into. As a woman I was submitting. I was conforming to the norms of society, largely formed in a patriarchal environment. I was completely, unconsciously unaware and moving fast into the negative. My inner child was driving the bus, and I was heading for a collision and in my unawareness I didn't even see it coming. However, my intuition was like a continuous nagging in the back of my mind, which was accompanied by an unsettling and unhappy feeling. But I didn't want to listen, because I was afraid of the implications – which would include ending my marriage, moving back to Dublin, and all the financial consequences of this.

My eagerness to please those around me was borne out of my own insecurities and conditioning. I was perpetually trying to look after other people's needs, always secretly hoping that it would eventually be my turn. I did hear my inner child calling me. She was telling me she was unhappy in her marriage and where she was living. She was also telling me she was sick of conforming to societal expectations. I was absolutely terrified of what she was saying to me. I desperately chose not to listen; I tried to ignore her and shut her up. This built resentment in me. It has been my experience that resentment is a clear indication that you are not looking after your own inner child.

All this was a result of my empathic nature and learned behavioural patterns. I did not just suddenly start to do this once I became a wife or mother. As a child I had always put others first. This is the essence of who I am. However, I had the sequence in reverse order. You have to look after yourself and your own inner child first. This builds a solid foundation for you and everyone else in your life. But this is not what I did at the time. I thought it would be selfish. I was trying to ripple from the outside in. I was miserably failing to get to my centre and I was going against natural law. This led me to the ripple effect – realising that the ripples always move from the inside out, not the outside in. This became my mantra, and it still reminds me to start with myself. It keeps me from abandoning my precious little inner child. Perhaps you will use it too. Or you can find something else that resonates with you.

I spent three years of not being tuned in, to varying degrees. Using my radio metaphor, if I was trying to set my radio station to 100FM, I was probably getting AM, not FM at all. I spent another three years moving tentatively – sometimes not so tentatively – into alignment, from being unconsciously unaware to consciously unaware. I knew I needed to do something but I didn't know what. I had created a life for myself based on setting my internal navigation system to other people's routes and not my own. Despite my best intentions it was all coming to a head. As a woman, I had succumbed to generations of conditioning. I had buried my ability, creativity and intelligence in order to conform. Now I had to tune myself in to my own frequency. I could not ignore the screams of my own inner child any longer. She had begun to throw all her toys out of the cot. Not only that, but I began to erupt externally too. I became irritable and very unhappy, I felt my own life was on hold and I was very frightened of the truth of my situation.

Now I found myself having to stand entirely in my own power, especially with regard to the social expectations and conditioning surrounding marriage. Before I could hope to find mutual empowerment with anyone else, I needed to find it within myself. I was journeying on the inside and that was making itself manifest on the outside. For the most part I was a married stay-at-home mum. I had moved from Dublin to Spain and then to the west coast of Ireland, but my internal navigation system was always pointing towards Dublin. It knew exactly where I should be and it was constantly whispering, 'Go back; you've taken a wrong turn.' Eventually I had no choice but to listen.

One day when I was living on the west coast of Ireland, I was driving into the village on my own, feeling as though I was sinking fast and nobody could pull me out. I was at one of my lowest ebbs. I stopped the car, pulled into the side of the road and got out. I was nearly bent double with emotional pain. The feeling was so unbearable I just couldn't drive the car. I knew at that moment that if I didn't follow my intuition I was going to die. I had to do something. But I didn't know what.

I was moving from being consciously unaware to consciously aware. Transitioning to this kind of personal awareness was very scary and in my case it meant big change. I had to face my little inner child and honour her needs. I had to pull myself out of what I had created. I had to listen to my intuition, the voice of Source Energy. I needed to take every aspect of my life apart and rebuild it. I knew I was beginning to create my reality now in more awareness, and I was terrified. The feeling of intense emotional pain was my inner child – she just couldn't take it anymore.

The internal moves manifested themselves in the external. I managed to find my way back to my home town of Dublin. Finally I had come full circle, not without causing absolute mayhem on the way. Much like in Kellie's story below, I just wanted to run and I really and truly tried. But there was no getting away from myself. Eventually I just had to stop and clean up what I had created in unawareness. Ironically I was back where I had left 14 years before. However, there was one major difference. I was now a divorced woman with three wonderful children. I didn't fill any social expectations at all. I was on my own. I had nowhere to live. I had no job, it was in the middle of the recession and I was broke in more ways than one. I was also part of the first generation of divorced women in Ireland. Brilliant, just brilliant. What do I do now? I had to stand in my own power and align myself with who I really was. Not the conditioned version. I was either going to sink or swim. I made the f*ck it decision to swim. This meant I had to be true to my own uniqueness in conjunction with that infinite intelligence within me.

ANDREW

Cast your mind back to the kite metaphor for a moment. Andrew had the strings of many kites in his hand: his desires, what he wanted to create in his life. His personal life purpose and his higher life purpose were always there. He couldn't see what some of his kites looked like yet, but he still held the strings. Andrew had the marriage equality kite firmly in his hand all along, but he didn't realise it. He had to tune himself in to Source Energy first, to get his own house in order and start fulfilling his own personal purpose before his higher purpose would reveal itself. The unique gift that Source Energy wanted to bring into the world required Andrew to align himself with who he really was first. Not the watered-down version.

Let us take a look at what Andrew had to do to align himself with Source Energy. Knowing he was gay but hiding it was, as he says himself, 'a complicated mess'. Despite being surrounded by loving family and friends, societal expectations were dictating to him how he lived his life. Andrew was faced with an internal struggle. He had two options. He could either align with Source Energy, or he could deny his true essence and try to align himself with society and all its requirements. He was sad, lonely and fearful. His sexual relationships were a total disaster and he was partying hard. Just like the Prodigal Son, Andrew was lost to himself. He spent years in this internal conflict. By the time he was in his early twenties it had reached fever pitch. Realising he was gay and denying this for the sake of society couldn't possibly work. It was at this point he had to take everything apart and rebuild his life in a different way.

He had come too far away from his centre. He was running away from that powerful presence inside him. Source Energy waited patiently for his return. The only thing that slowed him down, and will slow you down, is trying to escape from being true to yourself.

Gradually and more mindfully, he started to tune himself in, using acupuncture and yoga as tools to help him step toward alignment and heal himself. In moving toward alignment with Source Energy, Andrew agreed to take part in Rites of Passage, a large-scale public event produced by Kathy Scott of The Trailblazery. The Trailblazery is a cultural platform dedicated to creatively activating people and possibilities in Ireland. Partaking in this meant that Andrew was exposing himself openly to society by telling his story in public. As you can imagine, this brought up great fear.

Then he had to acknowledge the screams of his inner child, which he had ignored completely. He used a childhood picture of himself as a means of connecting to this child. Initially, as he pondered on the picture, he thought how much suffering that beautiful boy was going to have to endure. He also found it hard to relate to the image in the picture. Instead he treated the image of the child as a third party. He had kept his inner child so hidden that he didn't want anyone to see him. The child had been so wounded by his early experiences in life that Andrew was desperately trying to protect him. Andrew had become his own jailer, keeping himself locked away.

In doing so he was blocking the flow of his life and also blocking all his hopes, dreams and aspirations. Resistance from your fearful inner child is what prevents your kites coming in to land. Sometimes the inner child's fears are so powerful your desires never get a chance to come in.

Remember my mantra, 'the ripples always move from the inside out, not the outside in'.

During our work together, Andrew realised this inner child held the key, so he started to actively and mindfully love and nurture his child. During our sessions he was being brought into alignment with unconditional love and personal power. As Andrew was aligning the fearful inner child, that alchemy I spoke about earlier was beginning to take place. He began to see that his negative experiences were a way to move forward positively. He was now in the process of turning base metal into gold. During Andrew's sessions with me I could see the real Andrew unfold in front of my eyes. As he aligned he began to grow in his own personal power and strength. This began to radiate from him. It was wonderful for me to be able to hold that space for him, and watch as he began to release himself from the remainder of his self-imposed internal prison sentence.

In acknowledging his inner child and all the pain he had buried, Andrew started to release repressed feelings from years of being bullied. He needed to let these fears go. As he set himself free from gripping fear, he began to move forward. In doing this he gradually arrived at the point of alignment within him where the divine and the human meet. He had already acknowledged who he was, but this gave him the strength to step fully into his own personal power. By strengthening himself from the inside, he was beginning to ripple out to a wider audience.

In each session I coaxed Andrew to release the shackles of societal and generational repression and it was marvellous. He had to liberate himself first before he could help others do the same.

When you get stuck in the small, fearful picture you neither care nor want to see the bigger picture. You can barely look after yourself, never mind others, but, miraculously, when you align yourself with Source Energy all this changes.

Source Energy was now expressing itself fully through Andrew as a gay man. It disclosed itself through his sexual orientation. The world is in desperate need of equality, and Source Energy was calling Andrew to play his part. He was by now fulfilling his personal purpose, and this left him free to allow this magnificent energy to work through him for the good of humanity. There was important 'equality work' to be done and Andrew had to get out of his own way to do it. The gain of alignment is twofold – it is both for yourself and for others.

Pressing the fast forward button, we arrive in 2014 in the midst of a frantic lead-up to the marriage equality referendum. Andrew, as a director, had spent years working towards this. His intuition, which is the voice of Source Energy, called to him on many occasions. He was a social activist. It was in his blood. His ancestors were involved in the 1913 Dublin lockout and some had fought in the 1916 Rising. Andrew's parents had instilled a sense of equality and love in him, positive childhood conditioning that became the backbone of Andrew's mission in life and was a part of the formation of his higher purpose.

Andrew was now maintaining and using his alignment to deliberately co-create his own reality. He was beginning to fulfil his higher purpose, and using all his tools to help him stay balanced and tuned in. He was under no illusion about the enormity of the task: to land this referendum kite, it was imperative for him to stay aligned and focused.

I encouraged Andrew to ask for clarity on how to prepare for the referendum. His intuition guided him to take time off before all hell broke loose. Sometimes you can be too fearful to let go of the reins, so you just plough ahead, when you should first take time to prepare yourself. This is an important point. Your intuition tells you to stop and your fear tells you to panic and keep going. Andrew had the presence of mind to listen to his intuition, which guided him to a yoga retreat in Bali. Andrew didn't jump into the frenzy of the campaign; instead, he was making sure that he was powerfully aligned. We were clearing the path ahead of him energetically. He was like a fighter getting ready for a big fight. He needed to psych himself up.

To create anything it is vital to have energetic focus. Sometimes your creations require soft focus; at other times they need intense focus. Andrew was heading into a period of intense energetic focus. The marriage equality kite was now more visible than ever, and careering into reality. Many people tell me that they don't have time to meditate, but my experience is that you don't have time not to meditate, or align yourself in whatever way suits you. Meditating actually speeds things up.

Andrew had a session with me before he went to Bali to prepare him for his trip. I was paving the way for him to get maximum benefit from it. He also had a session when he came back to consolidate his experience. He was cleverly clearing the way for himself, energetically and mentally. This was a huge campaign, and Andrew was mindful that he needed to make sure he was internally strong.

In Bali Andrew had been meditating, softly focusing on infinite, unconditional love, and during one of these meditations he had an enlightening experience that resulted in an opening of his heart chakra and a sudden and intensely overwhelming feeling of unconditional love. This type of experience is possible when you are aligned. Andrew had already paved the way for this to happen.

Andrew began using this experience as another tool to keep himself aligned. During one of his sessions with me in the midst of the referendum campaign, we developed another tool for him to use. It was a mantra: 'release the outcome'. Andrew was now aligned and he knew and trusted what this meant. Source Energy is powerful, strong, unconditional love, limitless and abundant. When you merge with this kind of energy it begins to work for you and through you. You begin to embody and use all its attributes. You have to acknowledge this as part of who you are. Andrew was consciously aware that Source Energy was working through him. Therefore he also knew the outcome had to be good. He knew that, whatever the outcome of the referendum, everything had been irrevocably changed. Creating from Source Energy through alignment guarantees a positive result sooner or later. Andrew knew that the work was energetically done, and he could release the outcome because the higher purpose had already been achieved. This had yet to unfold in its entirety and is still unfolding.

This is a perfect example of how, in aligning yourself, your own life's purpose starts to be made manifest, and gradually, as you develop this, your higher life's purpose starts to unfold.

KELLIE

Earlier I mentioned how children do not move far from their alignment with Source Energy. They remain tuned in until conditioning and fear begin to take over. Using the radio metaphor again, some of us tune out gradually over a long period of time. For Kellie it was immediate and caused by deep shock and trauma. I shall relay her story in her own words giving you an idea of the many ways you can slip into unconscious unawareness, if you do not mindfully look after and practise staying aligned.

It began on a very wet October day in not so sunny Sydney. One of those days that the rain feels like it's never going to end, but in a slightly soothing way reminds you of home. We were due to drive up the coast to a holiday home some friends had rented for the bank holiday weekend. My boyfriend at the time was flying back from Melbourne that evening. He was picking me up, and the plan was to jump straight in the car and get on the road.

As I packed, I just couldn't help but feel that something wasn't right, in the type of way that you can't make any sense of because it's just a feeling you have. I tried to shake it off but when my boyfriend walked through the door I blurted out, 'I really don't think we should drive tonight'. I didn't know why. I just felt something was going to happen. It was dark and raining outside, I couldn't help thinking that we would drive off the road or something. My boyfriend took it in his stride and we decided to go in the morning instead.

So instead we went to a small Thai restaurant on Bondi Road while waiting for the torrential rain to stop. Tarantula rain, I sometimes call it, as it reminds me of spiders' legs dancing on the ground. When the rain stopped we left the restaurant. The restaurant was a stone's throw from where I was living. My then boyfriend needed something from the convenience store so he ran ahead while I waited to cross the road.

Looking right, no traffic, cross the mid-point line, looking left, no traffic. Then suddenly I'm flying through the air with this incredible force that came from the right but I've no idea what it was. All I could hear were the brakes of a car screeching on the wet surface, and I'm thinking I've just been hit by a car, or a bus, please don't be a bus. I'm on Bondi Road in Sydney and I cannot die here.

It felt like I was floating through the air, no pain, but my mind was going really fast. Then I landed on a bonnet and quickly bounced to the road landing on my right-hand side mostly, head last to hit the ground.

The driver of the car was panicking and saying, 'I thought you were dead' over and over and I'm thinking, 'Am I dead?' I can't feel any pain for some reason and no words would come out. In the next few minutes there was conversation between my boyfriend and the driver.

What I now know is that my intuition was telling me not to go anywhere at all. The unease in me was my intuition communicating with me. But when something seems silly to the logical mind, it's sometimes easier to go against it.

What happened that night set off a chain of events whereby I needed to come back home to Ireland. But when this wasn't your plan, it can be hard to accept that things are different and you've got to surrender. So I did come home and started to face what I needed to, that the accident had happened and that life was different now.

My plan, of course, was just a very quick pit stop in Ireland, be with family and friends, figure what the next life steps would be and get myself to London, quickly. Probably maximum three months, I thought, to have all of life figured out. This is when I met Judith.

Shock can have disastrous effects on a person's life if not dealt with appropriately. When I met Kellie she was still reeling from the accident. She was not grounded and she was desperately trying to align herself. This was extremely hard for her to comprehend as she was so used to being tuned in or near enough to it. I always think of our energy body like a piece of Waterford crystal glass: if we get a deep shock, the glass breaks and all the shards fly everywhere and we become very shaky inside. It was imperative that Kellie rebalance and bring herself back into more alignment, before proceeding further with her life. If she built her life on these shaky broken foundations, she was building on something that was sure to topple at some point.

Kellie was suffering from post-traumatic stress disorder, and her fearful inner child wanted to bolt, to run away to London and not face what had happened to her. This little inner child was terrified. Kellie recalls thinking, 'I can't stop, because that is not what you do.' The moment when she realised she had to stop was really scary for her. Her intuition was telling her to stay, see this through and heal, while her traumatised inner child was telling her to keep moving. She needed to rebalance and realign fully. Her body needed to heal and her inner child was terrified and desperately wanted to feel herself again.

In releasing the urge to run, Kellie had to slow down to go faster. This takes great courage. She had the strings of a lot of wonderful kites in her hands but just for the moment she couldn't see any of them. Metaphorically, the sky was black and her kites seemed to be tangled and knotted, if in the sky at all. It was an extremely tough time. It was at this point the traumatised inner child could have taken over her life. If Kellie had allowed this child to take over she would have been controlled by fear. Instead she pressed the pause button on her exterior life and started to step, painfully at first, inwards to heal mentally, emotionally and physically. She listened to her intuition and she resisted the urge to run away from herself.

Minor shocks that you experience daily can throw you out of alignment and create a 'wobble' in your energy field. By using your tools, such as deep breathing or meditation, you can realign yourself quickly.

When you suffer a major shock in your life you have to allow more time to balance your system and align yourself. Severe shock can affect you profoundly, physically, mentally and emotionally. When you suffer a bigger shock it is wise to use everything you can to bring yourself back to alignment. Meditation is a powerful tool in conjunction with speaking to a doctor or psychologist. Everything can be combined.

Kellie had left her life in Australia, she had given up her job and her relationship was over. She found herself back in Dublin and extremely wounded on all levels. She was living at home with her wonderful family, but felt she had taken a step back. She had no job; in fact, due to her injuries, she was not physically able to work. A lot of her friends were now married with children and she felt she wasn't on the same path. To make matters worse, because of the accident she found herself caught up in a court case in Sydney.

Difficult as it was, she accepted that it had happened and now she was going to see it through. All her focus was going into her healing. Her support network was vital. Her sister Ashley was greatly instrumental in this. Kellie wisely used all the tools in her toolbox. She used a mantra at that time to soothe her inner child. Her mantra was, 'become comfortable with the uncomfortable.'

During our sessions she tentatively brought herself back into alignment. She was aware at a deep level that she had many wonderful things she wanted to create in her life. She knew she had the strings of these kites in her hand. She held steady, she didn't run. She cleared the majority of the trauma from the accident while also stepping through a court case. At the end of all of this she was able to land some fantastic kites by staying true to who she was and not running away from herself. She stayed aligned with Source Energy.

Finding time to meditate

—

There was a point in my life where I just wasn't ready to meditate, so I used other tools. I brought myself gradually to it. Now I would not go through my day without meditating, such is its importance in my life. I meditate at least once a day for 20 minutes. Most days I will do a lot more. I will always find a sneaky few minutes to pop it in. I find it especially useful when I am working on a big project. Andrew used meditation around the time of the marriage equality referendum and uses it continuously in his life. Kellie also uses meditation daily as an integral part of her life.

I know a wonderful lady who, like a lot of people, finds it hard to sit and meditate. She is nursing her small baby at the moment and uses breast-feeding as her form of meditation. She brings herself into a more aligned state while feeding her baby. It could be mindfully walking in nature, painting or drawing, even sitting silently for a few minutes. These are all forms of tuning yourself in, and there is no right or wrong way – find whatever works for you.

'Your inner domain is where the divine
and the human meet ...'

When your mind is uneasy this will be communicated to every aspect of your being, affecting you spiritually, physically, mentally and emotionally. Meditation soothes a troubled mind. When you can calm your inner world, you bring calm to your external world.

Here is a visualisation meditation I use in my therapy room and seminars. It will bring you to where the divine and human meet in your inner domain. It is at this juncture you become aligned. With practice you can easily bring yourself there.

This meditation helps you to acknowledge your inner child. Maybe you find it hard to connect with your inner little one. One thing is for sure, the child is there. Every time you feel afraid, challenged, angry or upset, this is the child calling you. There is a frightened child in all of us, a child who feels it hasn't been heard. This child will follow you around all the days of your life looking to be validated. It wants to be set free and to play. You are now going to take responsibility for this child. You are its guardian. Nobody else is responsible for your child now, only you.

VISUALISATION: WHERE THE DIVINE AND HUMAN MEET

Just for a few minutes, sit, settle down and get comfortable. Pull a cosy blanket around you. This is your time now. Close your eyes, relax your body, listen to the ebb and flow of your beautiful breath, ebbing and flowing, ebbing and flowing, ebbing and flowing ...

Feel for any stress or strain in your body. Take all your worries and imagine placing them in a beautiful basket on a shelf beside you. Leave them there just for now.

Place your hand on your heart. Softly rub your heart with your hand. Comfort yourself. Listen to the gentle ebb and flow of your beautiful breath. Ebbing and flowing, ebbing and flowing. It is like the tide within you. Ebbing and flowing. Let this beautiful breath take you deep inside yourself.

As you go deeper, you begin to see or get a sense of a little child. This child is you. The child is so precious, vulnerable and innocent. The energy around this child is radiating pure love and is very clear. But you have been hiding this little one away. You haven't been letting her use her gifts and talents because of fear. This young child is very frightened and has no self-worth. She doesn't know how special she is.

You find yourself moving toward the child and gently you hold her hand. Look into her beautiful little face. Wholeheartedly explain that you are sorry for ignoring and abandoning her, for hiding her away. Whisper to her, 'I will never leave you again. I have decided to fully look after you now and I will never leave you again.' Tell the child, 'I am your guardian now. I am responsible for you. I promise you that you are allowed to use your gifts.' Tell her that she can use these gifts as much as she likes. Look into her little face and say, 'I promise you, from this moment on you are free. You are allowed to play and have fun.' Fully focus on the little child. Tell her she comes first from now on. Tell her you come first.

Pick up the little child in your arms and whisper, 'I love you. I love you.'

As you walk a while with your child in your arms you see in front of you a warm glowing light. You are drawn to this light. You are warmed by its glow and you can feel yourself step fully and freely into this light. You know you are completely safe. Feel that powerful energy support you. Feel yourself completely free. You are limitless and loved unconditionally. This light is abundant in health, wealth, joy and happiness.

Breathe this powerful energy into you. Breathe it into every cell in your body. Breathe it into every organ and gland in your body. Feel this powerful energy as it ripples out into your auric field. This energy penetrates your deep knowing. This energy infuses you strongly with feelings of health, wealth and joy. Feel that energy building momentum, rippling out from you to your family. Feel this powerful, strong energy rippling from you out to your friends. Gaining more momentum, this energy ripples out to all the people you work with. Feel this magnificent energy ripple on out to all the people you haven't yet met. This abundant energy is limitless and ripples into the earth and out into the universe. Breathe this universal energy back in to you. Breathe it in to every organ and gland in your body. Breathe it in to every cell in your body. Feel the universe within you. You are the universe. You are powerful. You are strong. You are abundant. You are an embodiment of where the divine and human meet.

Now, before you open your eyes, set your expectations. From now on that little girl inside you comes before anyone or anything else, and you will always listen to her.

TOOLBOX

Lighting a fire and sitting by it in awareness of its comfort

Metaphors

Comforting clothes and blankets

Talking to your inner child (hand on heart)

Support of family and friends

Art and listening to music

Meditation

Yoga, acupuncture, massage, physiotherapy

Walking in nature or wherever you feel comfortable

Use a mantra – a song or a quote; whatever works for you

DIARY PAGES

Think back ...

Just take a moment to look back at your childhood. I am sure you can remember someone shining a light for you. Even the smallest flicker of light can have the most profound effects, positively influencing a child. My love for nature was nurtured by my grandmother Mary, who would tell me all about wild medicinal herbs. To this day I make my own herbal tinctures, and I have passed this love onto my children.

1 What positive conditioning has affected you profoundly and what negative conditioning has strongly affected you?

....

....

....

....

....

....

2 What positive conditioning has been passed on through generations in your family and what negative conditioning has been passed on?

....

....

....

....

....

....

3 Can you see the rippling effects this positive conditioning can have and how it will stretch way beyond you in time through generations? Can you see where the negative effects have rippled out?

....

....

....

....

....

....

....

....

....

4 How do you think your conditioning is blocking your three desires coming in to land?

....

....

....

....

....

....

....

....

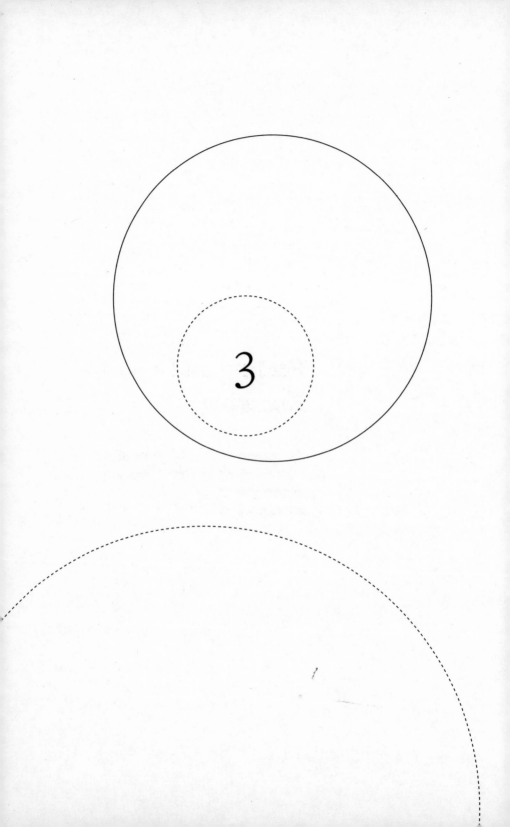

3

Feeling and Knowing

'Feel empowered. And if you start to do
it, if you start to feel your voice heard, you
will never go back.'

MARY ROBINSON

Tuning in

THROAT AND HEART CHAKRAS

Remember to take this time to align yourself. This is your private time to retreat to your inner domain. Take some of your favourite oils and rub them into your hands. Place your lovely face in the palms of your hands and breathe in the scent from the oil. Put some of the oil on your throat chakra. Or gently place one hand lightly over your throat; this is the area of self- expression. Place the other hand on your heart. What you feel and what you know is expressed through both the throat and heart chakras. Close your eyes. Now place soft inward focus on your heart, conjuring up the feeling of love. If you can, visualise the colour green. As you breathe, listen to your breath ebbing and flowing, ebbing and flowing, ebbing and flowing. When you are ready and at ease, continue to read.

What you will learn from this chapter

—

Let me prepare the way, creating a feeling of ease and anticipation around what you will find in the pages ahead. Reading the passage above will help you tune in and align with Source Energy before you start to read, which will make it easier to absorb the material. You are tentatively starting to use this hidden power within you more deliberately. In this chapter I will explain feeling and knowing, what a spark is and the loops you create in your life, unbeknownst to you. I will also be helping you to create new, more positive loops.

Then I will take you up onto the balcony and give you a bird's eye view of what you are really doing. After that you will start to mindfully create your own reality using the kite metaphor, imagination and visualisation. I will explain further how you can block your manifestations from coming in to land with resistance, or encourage them to come in by letting go of fear. This will clear the way for all your desires to land easily. Then of course there will be three more stories from Andrew, Kellie and me, followed by some useful tools for you to pick from. On your diary pages there will be empty spaces for you to fill in with your own words.

What is the difference between feeling and knowing?

—

First I will distinguish between 'emotions' and 'feelings'. They are related but do not mean the same thing. Let's get some clarity.

O Emotion is a physical response to an external cause or change.
O Feelings are mental experiences borne out of our brain's interpretation of the emotion.

O How you feel explains what emotion you are experiencing.

The distinctions I am using are based on the work of the neuroscientist Antonio Damasio. For example, the emotion of anger is a physical response to an incident such as a confrontation, argument, or disappointment. Your brain's interpretation of this is the feeling of wanting to scream, kick or roar.

Because emotions are physical and come in advance of feelings, you will get a strong sense in your body. Let's take anger as an example:

O Anger will promote blood flow.

O Your body will tense and your facial expressions will change.

O You may even get hot and bothered.

Your mental response to an emotion is a feeling. Feelings can therefore be quirky and bewildering at times. They are less straightforward than emotions. However, feelings can be insidious, creeping up on you over time and layering like an onion. This makes them difficult to understand and get to the root of. Emotions generally pass, while the feeling they have engendered can gather over a lifetime.

It is imperative in deliberately creating that you recognise what feelings you are conjuring up. When you can decipher whether it is a positive or negative feeling you can then choose which feelings you want to keep, and which you would like to get rid of. Knowing what feelings your inner child is attached to is very important here.

This may pickle your brain a little, but an emotion sparks a feeling and feelings spark emotions. Therefore, if you are creating a lot of negative emotions in your life you will create copious amounts of negative feelings. This means that you are creating your very own endless loop of negativity. If your inner child doesn't feel good enough or attractive enough, you will create this loop. If your inner child feels poor, this is the loop it will create. Getting to know what your inner child is really feeling is essential.

KNOWING

Knowing is something perceived as truth with conviction.

O To be cognitively aware is the mental action of knowing.

O This includes qualities such as perception, judgement and reasoning.

O It also includes anything that comes to be known through your intuition and knowledge.

O A feeling of calm intuitive determination is associated with knowing.

Imagine this scenario. You feel something is bothering your partner deeply. They are grumpy and angry all the time. Instinctively you know there is something wrong. But when asked they maintain everything is fine. It can be an uncomfortable feeling to know someone is struggling even if they will not openly verbalise it.

The five practices

—

If you create a lot of negative feelings, you will continue to do so. You are creating a loop. This is based on what I call the spark. In other words, it is a perpetual emotional chain reaction. The spark works like this. You have an emotion, it leads to a feeling, which leads to the same emotion, and on it goes in a loop.

Here is a little example of a chain reaction. As a child your parents never had enough money, and you grew up feeling the tension associated with lack of money. You conjure up these feelings of lack easily as you are familiar with the feeling. This leads to the same emotion of fear around money, leading to the same feeling of fear and on and on it goes it a lovely negative loop. All this means is you are creating fear around money, not creating money!

So that you don't spark endless loops of negativity, I would like to introduce you to the five practices and encourage you to use them in your everyday life, starting now. They will help you get vital information on what emotions, feelings and intuitions you are basing your life on. Remember, you are already creating your own reality. Unbeknownst to you, a large proportion of your reality is probably being created negatively through internal chat. Using these tools and practices will help you figure out what you are really doing and start to create sparks of positivity.

The five practices are:

1   I will practise standing on the balcony of my life. This means taking a step back and becoming the observer of my actions and reactions.
2   I will observe my thoughts, feelings, words, body language and actions.
3   I will look after my inner child. Hand on heart.
4   I will choose the emotions and the feelings I want to conjure up.
5   I will listen to my intuition, gut feelings or hunches.

Now let us look again at the money example from earlier on and apply the five practices. You now know you have created an negative loop around money. You are creating fear around money, not money itself. Taking a mental step back, you observe the internal chatter playing over and over in your head about money. This is your fearful inner child. Observe your body language and how you are feeling when issues of money arise. Then, when you have caught yourself playing the same old record in your head, put your hand on your heart and begin to internally talk to your fearful inner child. Acknowledge the inner child's fears first – don't ignore them or push them away. Then soothe the child. Gradually tell your inner child that you are now going to conjure up more a positive feeling; that you are open to creating something different. By doing this often and practising standing on the balcony you gradually change the constant negative chatter that is programming your subconscious mind. You are deliberately choosing more positive chatter that also programmes your mind. You are beginning to pick the emotions and feelings you want to conjure up.

Here is a saying to help you:

'Each day I will stand on the balcony and observe my life. I promise to look after my inner child hand on heart. I will then conjure up the emotions and feelings I choose while listening to my intuition.'

Write this down in your diary or on your phone. Stick it to your desk or beside your bed. This will remind you to do it. We have busy lives, our negative conditioning is deep, and it can be easy to forget. Reprogramming the subconscious mind takes repetition before it becomes automatic. It is a little bit like learning to drive a car: it's difficult at first, but after a short while it becomes automatic; you don't even think about it.

More about intuition

—

Intuition is closely connected to feeling and knowing. Let us recap how you know when it is your intuition calling and when it is your fearful inner child.

The fearful inner child's calling can be felt at all levels of your being:

O The fearful inner child feels insecure or anxious.

O You might have nervous or cramping feelings in the pit of your stomach.

O You might feel tension in your body or a panicky urgency in your chest.

O Your fight or flight response may be activated.

O There is an attachment to an outcome to such a degree that it causes severe anxiety and fear. (Please see a doctor if you are in any doubt.)

Intuition is the voice of Source Energy:

O It is accompanied by a deep sense of knowing and calm.

O Your body is relaxed. It is easier to recognise the intuition when you are working with Source Energy and you are aligned.

O You might refer to your intuition as your gut feeling.

O You can understand things instinctively.

O Intuition is an insight or hunch and it is strongly felt.

O When you get a strong intuition you have absolutely no doubt.

Listen to your intuition at all times. You will soon see the results in your life.

Imagination and visualisation

—

The importance of our imagination is greatly undervalued. Don't scoff at it. Einstein said that 'the true sign of intelligence is not knowledge but imagination', and Carl Jung suggested that our minds are led by patterns, images and thoughts that are a 'psychic system of a collective, universal, and impersonal nature'. Neurobiologist Gerald Hüther introduced the concept of 'inner images'. These 'inner images' are vital when you are creating your own reality in awareness.

Just as an artist creates an outline or picture in her head, before putting it onto canvas, you will use your 'inner images' to create what you want on your life's canvas. These 'inner images' are central to how you use and develop your brain. You are the artist and you are practising *the art of deliberately creating*. As a little child you were an expert at using your intuition, imagination and visualisation skills. However, these skills may have become a little rusty. Unfortunately society has conditioned you to 'grow up' and has encouraged the abandonment of personal imagination. Don't worry – with a little practice it will all come flooding back to you. Your inner child really wants to play.

Play and fun are crucial ingredients in creating your own reality. Keeping yourself aligned with play and fun is a sure indicator that you are aligned with Source Energy, allowing you access to the field of pure potential. So let yourself play, bring as much fun and play as you can into your life right now. Watch a silly movie. Dance and sing, even if it is in front of your own mirror. Try your clothes on, mixing and matching, dolling yourself up, if this is what you enjoy. It is the simple things in life that often bring a smile to our faces.

Feeling for resistance

—

You are an artist born to create, and you know what you want to create in your life. You have already had many desires and you are constantly thinking of new ones. Your desires can be a strong conviction within you, or they can hide from your conscious view for a while. Once the knowing or the desire presents itself to you it immediately starts to form. When you have a knowing or desire it instantly becomes a minute particle of reality. It is a reality in its tiniest and earliest stages. It needs to be nurtured carefully. It is wise to keep your fledgling creation or idea to yourself for a while.

This vulnerable and tender knowing represents a faraway kite. It seems way off in the distance. But once you have had the knowing or desire, you have the string in your hand. Sooner or later you will bring this knowing into hard matter. Provided you don't block it with fear and resistance.

This resistance is fear, your inner terrified child, and your child resists because of limited self-beliefs and conditioning. The child is conditioned not to believe in herself and her own creative ability. The child has forgotten to trust her deepest knowing and feeling. The kite of your creation or idea then becomes stuck, and the level of resistance determines the speed at which your creation comes in to land.

Seeing your idea forming and creating from beginning to end without fear is the true joy. It is the entire process of creating, from a minuscule knowing or feeling to full realisation, that is so enjoyable. By the time it finally arrives, the journey is nearly done.

'Flying your kite is the process of bringing your idea in from a tiny
speck of reality right into the physical world'

The ultimate aim is to create because you can, because that's who you really are. You are a co-creator with Source Energy. Source Energy is the creative force in and of the universe. It constantly creates, constantly expands. It is a creative force and that is what you are designed to do too; you create every second of your life. You are free to create what you like in joy without fear. If each one of us created in awareness with Source Energy the world would be an entirely different place. It would be filled with joy, happiness, hope and abundance. Instead, most of us create predominantly from a place of fear in unawareness.

You must feel for any resistance as you fly your kite. Flying your kite is the process of bringing your idea in from that tiny speck of reality right into the physical world. However, it is important to realise that, just like a kite, you have to allow your idea to dance and bob in the wind when it needs to. This is what forms your co-creation. This type of percolation gathers motion. You cannot just pluck this speck of an idea from the stratosphere of your mind and yank it into hard reality all in one fell swoop. Sometimes you need to pull on the string. At other times you will concede and let it fly, enjoying the process. When you feel the line in your hand you can ease the string, slowing the descent to ensure a soft landing.

A lot of people sense their creation as a speck in their mind's eye and instantly want to bring it to fruition. Depending on what you want to create and how good you are at it, this is not always possible. Sometimes you can create instantaneously, but sometimes your creations need time to incubate, to grow; when they are ready they will be born into this reality. It doesn't have to take for ever. The key is to keep aligning with Source Energy. Then apply soft focus to your idea and clear the resistance. This is mainly an internal process. A lot of people think they should be 'doing' something externally. That's not necessarily the case. Your own internal knowing and intuition will guide you to what you should be 'doing' externally. It takes far less 'doing' and a lot more feeling and knowing. Using your intuition to create your own reality is vital.

This is one of the reasons why meditation is so important. It clears the mind, allowing time for your kites to fly freely. As you meditate, you gently release any resistance, as if you were calming the weather on a blustery day.

Creating your own reality

—

Let's say you have an old car. Money is tight and you can't afford to change it. You are out driving and you can hear the fan belt squealing. You know it is not serious, but in that moment you make what I call a *f*ck it* decision. In that second you say inwardly, 'That's it. I want a new car, before this thing starts costing me more money. I'm going to change it.' At that moment the desire is set in stone within you. The new car has now become a particle of reality. The string of your kite is now in your hand. You cannot see the kite yet; it is still in the stratosphere. But it exists within you.

There are two ways of handling this new knowing. Bear in mind that a knowing is a deeply held feeling or conviction. The first scenario shows the resistances and blocks you might encounter within yourself and others.

SCENARIO 1: BLOCKS AND RESISTANCE
You go home and announce to your partner that you've had a brilliant idea – you're getting a new car. At that point everything goes pear-shaped. Just before you walked in the door your partner was sifting through loads of bills, worrying where the money was going to come from. In you

come, all chirpy, with your new, rather fragile yet wonderful 'particle of creation'. As you announce it with great gusto, the colour drains from your partner's face and all hell breaks loose. Shortly after this altercation you bin your idea. Limiting yourself, you revert to a feeling of lack due to other people's fears. I am not saying that you should go out and get a loan that will put you into more debt. What I am saying is that there is a feeling and knowing of lack that both parties involved are buying into.

It is imperative that you change internally the way you feel about money. Do not buy into someone else's fear or what appears to be reality. If you hold on to your idea and align yourself with Source Energy, gradually your external circumstances will change. Remember, your idea is a shred of reality. However, if you listen to the fears of someone else's frightened inner child you will never get anywhere. You will throw your shred of reality away. At this point you should remember who you really are. Creating with Source Energy is limitless. Creating with two frightened children is definitely limited.

SCENARIO 2: RELEASING BLOCKS AND KEEPING THE WAY CLEAR
After having your epiphany you realise that this is a possibility. You know who you are. You are a creator with Source Energy and you are limitless. All you need to do is stay aligned. Starting to play with your idea, you imagine your creation as a kite. It is in the distance. You have the string in your hand. The tug is your thoughts and imaginings about it. Realistically you haven't got the money. Your inner child is beginning to get a bit worried. Putting your hand on your heart you soothe the little child. Tell her you aren't sure yet how the money will come. But it will come. Tell her that you have the string firmly in your hand, and that's the most important thing. You are not going to lie to your inner child or brainwash her with unbelievable affirmations. Instead you are

going to lead her to the idea gently. Bit by bit she will start to believe it for herself. If you can think and believe it, you can have it.

'The lips of wisdom are closed except to the ears of understanding.'

THE KYBALION

The subconscious does not listen to unbelievable babble. It listens to how you feel. So you need to feel 'you can' before 'you can'; you need to feel wealth before wealth will come. All you know now is you are going to get a new car. You leave the kite to percolate. It needs time to form. This kite has yet to unfold and reveal itself so you need to keep this private for the moment. Listen to your intuition. Be careful of what you say and who you say it to. You don't want to attract other people's fears. This gives the kite a chance to land.

This is all done with your feeling and knowing. In awareness of what you are doing, you go home and sit to meditate. As you meditate you are clearing resistance around your kites. Clearing your mind gives you access to the field of pure potential. You are staying aligned and waiting for the voice of Source Energy to speak to you. This is your intuition. Listen to it. This is softly focusing inwardly. You are now beginning to create your own reality. By ignoring what you have already created externally, for example lack of money, and simply applying soft focus, using your kite visualisation and meditation as a tool, you begin to change everything from the inside out. It is simple and it really works, but you have to retrain yourself.

Before I tell you a story from my own experiences, let me remind you of the five practices:

1 I will practise standing on the balcony of my life. This means taking a step back and becoming the observer of my actions and reactions.

2 I will observe my thoughts, feelings, words, body language and actions.

3 I will look after my inner child. Hand on heart.

4 I will choose the emotions and the feelings I want to conjure up.

5 I will listen to my intuition, gut feelings or hunches.

Recognising your own fears and the fears of those around you enables you to release resistance. This is of great benefit when you are creating your own reality. The more resistance you put up, the more it blocks the way for your kites to land. No matter what you are creating, from a holiday in Bali to a campaign, you need to address your fears. Ignoring them will only cause more resistance, which will slow down what you want to bring in. This is where the five practices will come in handy.

JUDITH

I will give you an example from my own life. When I came back to Dublin from my rather emotional travels, I was completely financially broke. I needed to put down roots. As I said earlier, I needed to find schools for the children, a house to live in and a job. I was in big fear of money and the lack of it. So I began to mindfully align myself and that took the form of being in nature and walking a lot. This allowed me to listen to my deepest knowing. My intuition was guiding me to start a business and invest in what I needed for that business. Logically speaking, it would have made more sense to get a 'proper job'. However my intuition was guiding me back to opening up my practice again. I ignored my external circumstances as much as I could and using the processes I am outlining in this book, my practice gained momentum and grew rapidly.

However, last October something on the periphery of my private life affected my financial situation. I went into fear. This emotion of fear was very much based on past experiences. My subconscious was triggered and my inner child was shaken. I knew I was not aligned. I began to worry about money and fear gripped me. This time, however, I stopped and faced the fear. Florence Scovel Shinn has a saying, 'Face the lion and the lion runs away, run from the lion and the lion runs after you.' I faced the lion and for three days I stood intently on the balcony of my life and observed my behaviour. This type of intense focus was necessary. I did not want to create a negative pattern around money. I held my inner child as she went spiralling into old fear. I was constantly physically rubbing my heart with my hand to remind myself to look inward. It is a deliberate habit I formed to soothe my inner child no matter where I am. I knew I needed to keep myself aligned. I also knew I had to conjure up the feeling of wealth and abundance even though I didn't feel it.

My subconscious needed to feel plentiful. Abundance is health, wealth, joy and happiness. I was under no illusion – I had started to create a negative loop. The spark was ignited, the spark of a fearful emotion associated with money. This would invariably lead to the feeling of fear around money. Then back to the emotion and the chain reaction would continue. I needed to quickly quench this spark. Whatever happens internally will be manifested externally – this I knew. I am the creator of my own reality and I did not intend to create a shortage of money, particularly when things were going well.

For three days I focused internally and externally on bringing myself gently back from fear and into alignment. I meditated every day, sometimes twice a day. Meditation was clearing my mind. My meditations were allowing me access to the field of pure potential. I kept asking for guidance from that infinite intelligence within me. I set my intentions and asked for clarity. In order to hear the voice of Source

Energy – intuition – I had to ease my mind. I knew I would be guided. My job was not to panic or do anything much. My job was to stay aligned. I acknowledged and comforted my inner child. I did not scold her, ignore her or push her away. I talked to her. I soothed her. My mantra was 'I can do this'. When the negative thoughts and fears came up, which was every minute at the start, I knew this was my inner little girl. I kept telling her, 'I can do this. It's okay, I can do this.' I was observing and changing my negative chatter into positive chatter, not allowing it to take over and form a negative loop. My internal dialogue went something like this. 'Come here to me, pet, I will find a way, don't worry, I can do this. Just keep stepping, one little step at a time.' I was not allowing myself to create negative loops of fear; I was creating hope, allowing myself to stay tuned in. Affirmations will only bring you to a point. Creating positive internal dialogue with feeling influences the subconscious mind – remember, the inner child is the subconscious mind, and every few seconds of negative or positive chatter programmes it.

I used all the tools in my toolbox and formed more. I love walking and I used this as a way of easing my mind. I used it to keep me aligned. This was helping me to hear my intuition. I did not want my intuition to be overrun by my screaming, fearful inner little girl. It was autumn time and for three days I frequently walked the park. Inwardly I was standing on the balcony observing my behaviour. The first day into my self-observations I noticed my head was down and my brow furrowed. My body was not relaxed. The beauty of the autumnal park was going completely unnoticed. I was ticking all the boxes. I was using my tools. But I was trying too hard to align myself and it wasn't working. This would only lead to more fear and frustration. I was fooling myself. I started to scold my inner child, telling her she should know better. I berated myself. I wasn't practising what I was preaching. I was beginning to form another loop. It was a negative loop. I was creating another spark to put out.

I stopped. I felt panic in my body. I sat on a park bench and closed my eyes. I didn't care if passers-by thought I was mad. I knew what I was doing. While my eyes were closed I began to breathe more deeply. I scanned my body for the areas that were tense. I allowed my body to relax. I had my hand on my heart in solidarity with my inner child. I inhaled the fresh autumn air and I listened to the birds for a while, allowing them to take me inwards. Then I visualised a wicker basket (I love wicker), put all my worries in it and popped a lid on it. Then I put the basket with the worries on an imaginary shelf. I had shelved the fear. I told myself I would go back to the basket after my walk. By doing this I had given myself a little break, just for a few minutes. My knowing was that it would all be there on the shelf waiting for me when I went back to it. That is, if I wanted to go back to a basket full of worries.

Nowadays when I do this visualisation I imagine my basket of worries dissolving into a puff of smoke. It is worth noting that the subconscious doesn't know the difference between what you imagine and what is real, once you believe, feel and know it. The more you practise and use these tools the better you get at it. You can positively programme your subconscious mind, and then the new programme will become an automatic response.

After my visualisation I walked and continued to breathe deeply. Because I was more relaxed and my worries were shelved for the moment, I took in my surroundings. I began to see the abundance in nature and started to feel hope, which was better than fear. I was still observing myself and I knew that my lift in mood would start another spark. This time the chain reaction was a positive one. It was only a glimmer but it was all I needed. I just needed to keep on feeding this positive spark. All the beech nuts and leaves strewn everywhere reminded me of how abundant nature is. It also brought me back to my senses. It reminded me that I too am a part of nature. This was going to be my tool to conjure up abundance. I laughed to myself. I had quietened my mind. I had asked for guidance. Then the intuition of what to do next came to me. It was easy when I stopped feeling afraid long enough to listen.

I had felt the feeling of abundance in the pit of my stomach. I needed to feel that, not fear. This was the spark that I was going to use to create more abundance. I was going to use the park and all its abundance to make me feel abundant. I was going to keep conjuring up that 'park' feeling over and over again. I was not going to allow myself to conjure up the feeling of fear. Once you can feel it on the inside it has to be made manifest on the outside. So for two days after my walk in the park I just kept on conjuring up that feeling. As I fed the abundant feeling and not the fearful one, I could feel it growing inside me. I could also feel the fear subsiding. Over the days that followed my confidence grew and my mantra of 'I can do this' changed to 'I am doing this'.

We are very conditioned to take notice of the negative emotions such as fear and anger. It is easy to conjure up these emotions. It becomes second nature for us to feel them. It has become our automatic response. The pity of whipping up these feelings regularly is that you are creating your own reality from negativity. If they are negative feelings they will produce negative results. If you plant a potato, a potato will grow, no matter how much you would like a rose to grow.

I had successfully conjured up abundance. I was aware that focusing on the abundance of nature and feeling it within me would bring not only wealth but health, joy and happiness too. I knew that joy would bring me into alignment with Source Energy. I was in the early stages of a flow again. With this alignment, I knew all things were possible from this place within me. Source Energy is limitless. I looked forwards with anticipation to seeing the results, trusting the outcome. So much so that many wonderful ideas came to me. That included the idea that would lead to writing this book only a few short months after that experience.

This was something that worked for me because of my love of and connection to nature. You can use whatever makes you feel abundant. I particularly like feeling abundant because this is a feeling of health, wealth, joy and happiness.

A simple example of conjuring up a feeling is wearing nice clothes. This helps to instil positivity. It is good to put on something nice and feel good. Now use this properly as a tool in awareness. Conjure up the feeling of 'feeling a million dollars' not just 'looking a million dollars', whether you're wearing designer clothes or clothes from the charity shop. It is not the clothes per se, it is the feeling that matters.

It is imperative to stand on the balcony and observe your life. See what emotions and feelings you are conjuring up. Make sure they are positive abundant ones. It takes a bit of work to identify feelings.

The purpose of conjuring up feelings from the memory of the feeling is so that you can reignite this from within. Then you can use these positive feelings to create your own reality instead of using negative ones. It is mindfully choosing what feeling you want to create. Do you want to create a feeling of wealth or poverty? A feeling of love or hate? It is entirely up to you. Once you establish the feeling within you, for example abundance, practise conjuring it up until you get very good at it. Then it will simply have to be manifested in your life. More often than not we are experts at conjuring up negative feelings, for example anger, as we saw above. You can hold yourself in anger expertly and create from this point too. However, your creations will be limited and will always have a negative outcome. Remember, your subconscious mind will do exactly what your conscious mind tells it to do, whether positive or negative.

There are many different reasons for, and ways of, conjuring up a feeling. Let's take a look at how Andrew did it.

ANDREW

As Andrew was co-creating and co-managing the marriage equality campaign he was creating his own reality from the inside out. He was staying aligned with Source Energy. During our sessions he was learning how to tap into his deepest knowing while using feeling and intuition to guide him. The predominant feelings Andrew conjured up over the campaign were equality and love. Andrew used his profound sense of equality as a tool to create. Andrew refers to this as his deep inner awareness of knowing that something had to be put right.

When mapping out how acutely this feeling of equality had affected him, you would have to start with his family line. Generations of social activism ran through his veins. What solidified this strong feeling of social responsibility was his personal suffering – as a child he was persecuted for his then-perceived sexual orientation. Equality was imprinted in his

DNA, a feeling and knowing he could not deny. This feeling and knowing eventually lead him to do a masters in equality studies at UCD's Social Justice department. It became easy for Andrew to conjure up the feeling of justice and equality for all. He had programmed himself to do it.

As Andrew aligned himself to Source Energy during the campaign, he had two predominant mantras. One was 'you can do anything now'. He was conjuring up the feeling of limitlessness inside himself. He would write it on yellow Post-its beside his bed and repeat it in the morning when he woke up. The mantra reminded him that through equality he could do anything. At a deep-rooted level his subconscious had felt that he couldn't do as others did. Now, through his alignment, he was changing that feeling deep within himself. He was reprogramming his subconscious mind with repetition.

Many of Andrew's colleagues were also beginning to feel their self-worth, and this empowered them. This type of positive feeling and knowing, emanating from the centre of so many people, had to make itself manifest on the outside. Andrew and his colleagues had collectively sent out the same desire. The reason this kite was pulled in so quickly and powerfully was because so many people had the same feeling and knowing. They were all working together to pull the kite in. Collectively they were conjuring up a feeling and it was powerful. So powerful, in fact, that it caused a momentous shift in the mindset of Irish society and indeed the world.

During the referendum and while keeping himself aligned, Andrew practised standing on the balcony. He did this by observing himself and others; by releasing the outcome and trusting Source Energy entirely. Andrew observed his fearful inner child. He got the opportunity to recognise this child within himself and within others. When dealing with difficult people and difficult situations Andrew was able to get on the balcony and see the bigger picture.

Andrew maintains the referendum was 'no Disney story', and I can well imagine it was very tough at times. The marriage equality campaign evoked huge negative responses from some people. Andrew was able to understand that homophobia caused huge fear and anxiety. By staying on the balcony and relating to the fearful inner child of those surrounding him, he was able to transform that fear. He did not succumb to it. Fear is like an infectious disease. It will spread like wildfire if not quenched.

Andrew needed to transcend his own fears in order to help others with theirs. Standing on the balcony, Andrew was able to recognise fully the struggle of being gay in Ireland. This was the pain of being rejected. It was a battle against being branded a second-class citizen and being ridiculed. However, he could also see what generations of societal conditioning had done to provoke such ardent fear in those who vehemently opposed the marriage equality campaign. Through standing on the balcony and reconciling with his own fearful inner child, Andrew was able to stay aligned with Source Energy.

He placed intense focus on staying on the balcony, and eventually it became his automatic response. So much so that a colleague at work noticed and said, 'When people challenge you, you take a step back and take a breath.' She asked him what he was doing. When Andrew was challenged by someone, he would ask himself, 'Is this my fearful inner child or is it their little child?' If it was his child he acknowledged it and took responsibility. He provided the inner child with support to heal and soothe, much as a parent would protect and help their child.

As he said himself, 'If it was my inner fearful child I had to take an even bigger step back.' If it was someone else's fear, he recognised what he was dealing with. Then he handled it with compassion from his adult self. This type of intense focus minimises conflict and resistance, and maximises the process of moving forward. He was doing this in full awareness of keeping the pathway ahead of him clear. Andrew and his co-creators had a big kite to land.

KELLIE

We'll stay with the kite metaphor for a while to explain how Kellie used feeling and knowing to her advantage. In her hand she had the strings of some kites that were negative: post-traumatic stress was one; a court case in Australia another. Kellie's life was put on pause. She had to land all these kites and they were not the kites she was used to landing. They were negative and Kellie, for the most part, did not operate that way in her life. That is one of the reasons why she listened to her intuition and didn't go to London. She knew deep down she would be trying to get away from her own self and that was never going to work. 'I've never been the type of person that has a five year plan. But I go with the flow and with what I feel is right. But I knew that I had to stop and that was the right thing to do.'

In fact Kellie did have a plan, a plan that was in alignment with Source Energy, one that normally allowed her kites to come in unrestricted. However, this time there was a lot of turbulence.

At this point I was helping Kellie to feel her way through the fog that had descended in her life. She used her intuition when she couldn't see clearly to decipher what kites were coming in to land. She felt her way. Gently she managed to isolate her negative kites, identifying that they needed to come in as easily as possible, without creating more drama around them. Then, slowly, while coming into more alignment and not running away, she began to get a feel for the other kites that were coming in on the back of these negative ones. She felt the resistance of her inner child, but did as much as she could to comfort that child. 'When I came back to Dublin I did think, okay, I have done the production side with TV commercials and short films, but I would love to do something similar in music.'

Earlier I mentioned that the moment you have a desire you form a connection and that connection is irrevocable. Well, her desire was to do something in the music business and the moment she thought it, it became a string in her hand with a fabulous kite at the end of the string. Kellie had popped that in. You actually do create instantly in the recesses of your mind first. Remember, once you have had the thought it is a small particle of reality. During her sessions with me we were gently creating momentum around her fledgling desire. But for the moment Kellie couldn't even see what shape or form it was going to take; it was too far out in the stratosphere.

Kellie's intuition was extremely keen. She knew instinctively that she had other strings of better kites in her hand, and because of this awareness she started tentatively to place soft focus on them. Even amid all the negativity she knew there was something better coming and she held on to that. Kellie was innately aware that she had to step through the post-traumatic stress and the court case. If she did that she could get to the good stuff. So she began to release resistance and she stopped fighting what she had to do. But that didn't stop her placing soft focus on what was percolating away in the distance. Whatever it was, it was just waiting for everything to clear.

I started meditating a lot and that is the one tool that I could use every single day. I would wake up anxious every morning. First of all I was back in Ireland when all the legal stuff was going on in Sydney. You are dealing with time differences and constantly feeling that it is never going away. I was sitting with it and being still and accepting that this is what had happened, and not resisting it. I just kept stepping through it one step at a time.

Kellie was staying on the balcony of her life as much as she could, observing her life, how she was feeling and what insights she was getting. As she was letting go of her resistance to staying in Ireland and step through what was going on, she was actually speeding up the process. She trusted her deepest knowing, despite the fact that on the outside her life seemed very blocked. She retreated more from the outside world to place focus on her internal world. This is something you should put into practice in your own life. Don't pay too much heed to the external circumstances, as these are already created. In order not to form a loop and keep creating what you are experiencing in your outer life, focus more on your intuition, meditate and receive guidance from within.

Kellie was aware that she could not just pluck her new, more positive kite from the stratosphere; she was also aware of a process and an order to things. She knew she had to land the negative kites first. But she also knew not to resist. What was created was created and would have to play itself out. But she could direct and decide how she was going to conduct herself through it. This she did with grace. She stayed aligned with Source Energy and followed her feeling, intuition and knowing.

VISUALISATION: THE WORRY BASKET

Allow yourself to play and let your imagination flow. Close your eyes for a moment and listen to the ebb and flow of your breath. Ebbing and flowing. Ebbing and flowing. Feel your body becoming more relaxed. Relax your eyes and ease your shoulders. Feel for any tension in your stomach area. Let the anxiety go. Now bring your attention to your legs and feel for any muscle tightness. Let this go. Feel all the stress and tension in your body dissolve. Put your hand on your heart and feel for your little inner child. Know your child is there waiting for you. Visualise a beautiful basket in your hands. This is the worry basket. Ask your lovely child to put all her worries and fears into it. Now imagine a shelf beside you. Tell your child you are going to put the worry basket on this shelf and leave it there just for now. Tell your inner child she is safe. You are minding and loving her.

Now think of a time in your life when you were happy and felt loved. It could be the love of a pet when you were a child, or a loving parent, grandparent or friend. Whatever your memory is, allow yourself to feel this memory deeply and start to conjure up the feeling. Breathe this feeling in. Breathe that happy, loved feeling into every cell in your body. Feel it ripple into your energy field around you. Feel that powerful feeling ripple out from you to the people you love. Place your hand on your heart and sit with your inner child and tell her you are minding and loving her.

TOOLBOX

Listen to your deep feeling and knowing

Practise conjuring up a feeling of abundance or love

Listen to your breath to soothe you and comfort your inner child, hand on heart

Don't forget about the five practices

Use your mantras

Make yourself feel good in small ways, for example, by wearing a lovely scarf or using your beautiful oils

DIARY PAGES

1 How are you feeling about your three desires? Are you feeling positivity or negativity around them? Write down a few positive lines on each desire.

2 Put your hand on your heart and ask your inner child to give you clarity, quickly and easily, about how to land your kites. Write a few lines about this clarity. It may come straight away or during the day, and it may come in stages or all at once.

....

....

....

....

....

....

....

....

....

....

....

3 Remember to listen to your intuition throughout the day and follow it. By following your intuition you are pulling your kites in to land.

4

Decisions and Expectations

'You are not stuck where you are unless
you decided to be.'

WAYNE W. DYER

Tuning in

THE SACRAL CHAKRA

Just take these few minutes to yourself. Light your candles and put on your oils. You have looked after everyone else all day and now it is the turn of your own inner child. Place your hand on your heart, gently rub your heart and connect with your inner child. Release any tension in your body. Bring your attention to your sacral chakra below your navel. This chakra is associated with desire. Close your eyes and softly decide to focus on this area, while gently visualising the colour orange. Listen to the ebb and the flow of your beautiful breath, ebbing and flowing, ebbing and flowing, ebbing and flowing ...

———

What you will learn from this chapter

—

In this chapter I will be helping you to conjure up feelings from positive memories. This will help you to access and direct your subconscious mind. I am constantly using the tools it loves, such as meditation, the inner child, metaphors, visualisations and imagination. I will also be introducing you to, and encouraging you to make, *f*ck it* decisions. So right now, place your hand on your heart and make your first *f*ck it* decision with feeling.

Say out loud, '*F*ck it*, I have decided to absorb the information given here easily and use it in my everyday life.' Again say out loud, '*F*ck it*, what have I got to lose?' Laugh, be empathic and be a bit bold. Just say '*F*ck it*.' By now you will have gathered that this chapter is all about decisions and expectations. You are becoming consciously aware of the power of positive decisions.

As your mind soaks up this chapter, you will realise that what you expect is what you create. If your expectations are limited, conditioned or fearful, that is what you will create. These limited expectations can be caused by societal, cultural and generational conditioning. You are now making a *f*ck it* decision to release that conditioning. I will be using a metaphor about technology to emphasise how the computer of our own human mind connects to the vast one-mind of Source Energy.

You will come to understand that updating your files on the internal computer of your mind is of paramount importance. I have included some helpful tools to encourage you to keep stepping and I have created a beautiful visualisation which will help you to download the silver cord connection. In your diary pages I will be asking you to make some more *f*ck it* decisions.

What is a *f*ck it* decision?

—

A *f*ck it* decision is emphatic. It is an epiphany, an 'Aha!' moment. It is a moment of sudden and great revelation and realisation.

O It is an absolute '*f*ck it*, I've had it!'

O You may have to get a big shock before you make a *f*ck it* decision.

O Or you might make a *f*ck it* decision in complete desperation.

'*F*ck it, f*ck it*, I've had enough.' How many times have you said those words? '*F*ck it*, why is it always me?', '*F*ck it*, I am sick of this.' You generally resort to such language when you are completely exasperated. Normally what follows these words is a decision. '*F*ck it*, I've decided that is never going to happen to me again.' Or '*F*ck it*, I've decided to change how I do this in future.' I am sure you can think of many times when you said this, or something similar, followed by a decision. *F*ck it* decisions are emphatic; they generally happen when you have been pushed too far. They are priceless decisions by virtue of the fact that they carry with them a big punch and powerfully influence your subconscious mind. However, you really don't have to be pushed to such lengths before you make a *f*ck it* decision.

If you are very poor at making decisions this will lead to very poor 'stop-start' momentum. Staying indecisive creates a block in bringing in and landing your desires. These blocks slow down the process of positively creating. Instead they create momentum around indecision, that's all.

Every morning I set my decisions for the day. I have trained myself into this habit. I do it when I wake up, before I get out of bed. I decide that I am in full health, wealth, joy and a whole host of other things. I am consciously directing my subconscious mind. I take every opportunity I can throughout the day to make decisions about the big things and the small things, and that's it – once I make them they are in. There is one major ingredient when you are doing this: feeling. The reason why a *f*ck it* decision is so powerful is because you normally say it with great feeling. It is the feeling that impresses the subconscious. Therefore I conjure up a *f*ck it* feeling. It is hard to express the feeling in words; that's why I use the term *f*ck it*. I conjure up an emphatic, strong, clear, bold feeling. I feel it. It is the feeling attached to the decision that directs my subconscious mind. Remember, this can be any feeling, for example a feeling of health, wealth, joy or happiness, or a feeling of self-love, self-worth or security. It is the feeling associated with what you want to create.

For example, every morning you wake up and dread going into work. Your boss micromanages, is harsh and undermines you. You are reacting to his poor management skills and you are losing confidence in your own abilities. Day by day things are getting worse. Your lack of confidence leads to errors and fear, which leads your boss to not fully trust you. You and your boss have now created a negative loop. Then you decide, '*F*ck it*, I'm going to create my own reality around this.' You think, '*F*ck it*, I need to get my confidence back' and start to conjure up feelings of confidence and self-worth. You comfort your inner fearful child. You remind yourself that you didn't always feel like this and that you *are* good at your job.

When you focus your thoughts on negativity you are on dangerous ground. Your conscious mind directs your subconscious mind, basically telling it what to do. If you feed your mind with negative thoughts or constant negative chatter, you will in turn receive negative emotions, feelings and memories. This will create momentum and endless loops of negativity. Then this will be manifest in your physical reality.

You have the ability to decide what thoughts you think. Simply by observing your internal chatter and monitoring your thoughts you will get valuable insight into the areas of your life you need to address. Remember that your conscious mind has the ability to direct your sub-conscious. This is a very powerful tool. When you align your mind with the one-mind of Source Energy the power is amplified.

Expectations

O An expectation is a strong belief that something will happen.

O What you expect, you create.

O Our expectations are greatly influenced by our upbringing, learned behavioural patterns and generational conditioning.

For example, during the dark days of economic crisis in Ireland in the 1980s, the majority of people grew up with mass unemployment and emigration. Generally there was little expectation around money, because most people didn't have any. However, if you grew up during the Celtic Tiger boom there was loads of money and you grew up expecting more.

Another example of this type of social and generational conditioning relates to self-worth or self-esteem. If you expect everyone else to be better then you, that is how you feel. Remember, the subconscious creates your reality from how you feel. So if you expect not to have any money or if you expect everyone else to be better than you, that is what's going to happen. Each morning when I set my decisions for the day, I fully expect what I decide to happen. There is no room for doubt.

When people try this initially they become disheartened as the results can be slow. This is only because you need to create momentum, practise your decisions and set them strongly with feeling. Then you need to release the resistance, which includes doubt. You also need to truly expect your decisions to materialise. Start off small and then build up to the big things. It's like a muscle. When you go to the gym you don't expect to be lifting the big weights first, but you do expect to be able to lift them in time.

SOCIETAL EXPECTATIONS AND SOCIAL NORMS

O Deciding to own who you are is the first step. Society has conditioned you, whether you realise it or not.

O Women and men see themselves defined through generations of misguided understandings.

O Gay people are expected to be straight.

O Women and men are expected to stay in unhealthy relationships.

O Some men expect to earn more money than women.

O Some women expect men to provide for them.

O Children are expected to go to college and follow family traditions.

O People are expected to get married first and then have a child.

O People are expected to work hard and struggle to earn a living. (These ceilings of limitation can be your biggest obstacle to creating wealth and happiness in your life.)

The list is endless, and all these expectations are coming from the outside in. What do you expect in your life, and what has been expected of you? More often than not, you end up doing what society expects you to do and not what you want for your own life.

Deciding what you want in your life, from the small things to the big things, then expecting them, actually sows seeds in the womb of your mind. These seeds gain momentum and grow. If you do not resist them with fear and doubt then they will be borne out in reality.

I remember one very talented lady who had plenty of wonderful ideas but who really needed to leave her very demanding job and work for herself. It would mean relying on her husband to support her until her business started to gain momentum.

> *I feel that my f*ck it decision is to leave my job. I feel like my decision has given me such a release and I feel finally I am listening to myself. It's terrifying for me to release my independence.*

She was brought up not to be reliant on a man. Therefore it was terrifying for her to step forward and make the *f*ck it* decision to leave her job and create her own business.

You can see very clearly how this woman's inner child is going into fear. She had been conditioned by society to think it wasn't wise to rely on a man, even though her wonderful husband didn't have a problem supporting her until the business took off. This fear is nothing to do with her present moment. This fear came from generations of conditioning. Women traditionally stayed at home, gave up their jobs and became reliant on their husbands. In doing so they quite often handed over their personal power to their husbands and in due course encouraged their daughters never to do the same.

Many women who choose to be stay-at-home mothers have undervalued their roles. This causes a ripple effect. If a woman undervalues herself she will be undervalued. This is creating momentum around negative self-worth issues and ripples through the generations.

The conscious mind directs the subconscious mind and tells it what to do. The trick is to make the subconscious feel it. Use the memories your subconscious has stored in your memory bank to conjure up a positive feeling. Use your senses to help you. For example, the smell of freshly baked bread might give you a feeling of your granny's house when you were small, or sitting beside the fire conjures up a feeling of warmth or security, both internally and externally. You don't necessary need to smell the bread or sit physically beside the fire. You can evoke those feelings inside you from memory.

The supercomputer

—

By now you are well used to my metaphors and visualisations. Your subconscious absorbs information much easier this way. Imagine Source Energy as a vast supercomputer storing all the universal files. This storage system is a container of information, storing everything imaginable, right down to your personal files. This supercomputer allows you to easily access and download information. Source Energy is the supercomputer, much like the cloud that we are familiar with in today's technological world. Just as the cloud is a remote server that manages and stores information, Source Energy holds the universal files in the same way. When we create with Source Energy we plug in and download from this supercomputer. Your conscious mind has access to this supercomputer at all times.

Just as your personal computer, phone or other devices can access the cloud at any time and download information immediately, you can access Source Energy in the same way. When you decide to align with Source Energy, you tune yourself in, emit a signal, and Source Energy automatically responds.

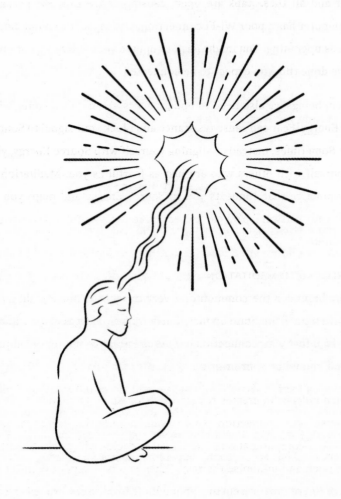

'When you decide to align with Source Energy you tune yourself in,
emit a signal, and Source Energy will automatically respond'

However, you know yourself that when you have too many tabs open this will slow your computer down. Let's say that you have ordered a takeaway, checked the time of your bus, lodged money into your friend's account and all these tabs are open, causing congestion. Or perhaps your computer has a poor Wi-Fi connection. Or maybe it's an old model and needs upgrading. You might need to update your software, but once you have done this you expect to be connected.

As human beings we also need to update our 'software' by aligning with Source Energy. Fear can cause resistance and block your signal to Source Energy. Sometimes, instead of aligning yourself with Source Energy, you sync yourself with others who are just as fearful as you. Meditation is the key practice that connects you to Source Energy and helps you to upgrade your software. You can expect to connect to this energy when you meditate.

ROAD BLOCKS TO MEDITATION

You may be under the common and very misguided illusion that you don't have time to meditate. In fact, you don't have time not to meditate. Making sure that your connection to Source Energy or the supercomputer is clear should be your priority.

Too much indecision creates resistance, 'stop-start' momentum, which slows down your connection. This is similar to having too many tabs open on your computer at once. You need to decide which tabs you want to leave open and minimise the rest. When you have a poor connection to Source Energy you are cutting yourself off from this powerful signal.

JUDITH

I would like to share with you an everyday example of how you can use your *f*ck it* decisions and expectations. I can think of many bigger examples, but you need to be able to apply these processes in your everyday life and it is very good practice for the bigger things. To give you a little bit of background, I was in work one day on a Thursday, and my appointment book had been completely full all week. I had college exams that Saturday and a thesis to submit, also on Saturday. I had a meeting with the publisher about this book the following Monday. I was sitting in my lovely treatment room in between clients and I was beginning to feel overwhelmed.

All my processes went out of the window and I started to spiral into fear. The internal negative chatter had begun. 'How am I going to get it all done? Sure, I have the thesis done but it needs to be perfect. I still need to study that last chapter for the exam, and what about that other chapter? I've only glanced at that one.' My body was beginning to get very tense and my shoulders rigid. I was becoming impatient and flustered. I felt restricted by time. It was at that moment I realised that my lovely fearful inner child was now running amok. There was no deliberately creating my own reality in awareness; there was only my inner child regurgitating old patterns. My subconscious had been triggered.

It was a mixture of my childlike interpretation of my school environment and conditioning. Fear of not being good enough and getting overwhelmed with a perceived time restriction was gripping me. In that moment I was a child afraid of 'getting into trouble' and feeling that everything had to be perfect. I was now seeing my life through the eyes of a six-year-old and, worse still, operating from a six-year-old's perspective.

Going back to my computer metaphor there were too many negative tabs open and they were slowing down my connection with Source Energy.

FIRST:

O I stopped.

O I stood on the balcony, caught my negative internal dialogue and observed my behaviour.

O I deciphered what momentum I was creating (more about momentum in the next chapter).

O I then made a *f*ck it* decision to stop creating negative momentum around time restriction and negative self-worth issues.

Remembering my mantra, 'the ripples always move from the inside out', I knew that if I continued in this vein, the negativity would ripple out into my life. This would start with my next client, who was due in a few minutes. Unless I aligned my energy, this client was not going to get as good a session as I would like.

It would lead me on to being distant and removed from my children when I got home. It would cloud my judgement over my thesis. I would try to cram for the exam and probably stay up all night. Then I would be exhausted for the exam and not be able to think at all or access any information from my weary brain. Never mind the negative momentum I would create around my lovely fledgling book. Or the type of energy it would emit to you, the reader.

O I needed a fast solution.

O I had to slow down to go faster.

O I had to calm the doubt and fear.

I was too wound up to meditate so I needed to rein myself in gently. I sat with my hand on my heart and immediately started to acknowledge my inner fearful child. I completely identified with her. I talked to her and was acknowledging, understanding and comforting. I am very comfortable with my inner child now so my language with her is soft. To give you an example of my internal dialogue it would go something like this: 'Come here to me, stop winding yourself up. You are okay; you can't really get it wrong; just pace yourself step by step.' It takes just a few seconds of this positive chit-chat to start to reprogramme your mind (or negative chit-chat – it's up to you).

I was mindfully bringing myself to a better place. I was easing the negative momentum I had created using the tool of the inner child. This takes practice but, just like driving a car, it will become an automatic response in time.

SECOND:

When I had soothed myself, I began to meditate, softly focusing on aligning my mind with the one-mind of Source Energy. Gently I connected my limited internal computer with the vast supercomputer, Source Energy. I cleared my mind and slowly, as I released my fear, I could feel that relaxed state, which is common when you connect with this energy, wash through me. I started to relax and become clear. I was beginning to see a better way of doing things and my mood had lifted. I had hope. In effect I had managed to minimise and close some of those negative tabs, aligning myself and speeding up my connection with infinite intelligence.

THIRD:

As I came out of my meditation I was aware that this was a prime time to set my *f*ck it* decisions and expectations around my work and what I would like to achieve in the coming few days. I decided to play with this a bit and almost laughed at my audacity. Just as fear and doubt slow down your creations, joy and play speed things up. I knew what I was doing. I was now creating positive momentum and I wanted to build on this.

I realised that my mind can compute as fast as it likes – the only limit it has is the limit I put on it. I decided to direct it and fully expect the desired outcome. I decided to deliberately focus on what I wanted to create, thus deliberately creating. I was emphatic that I was going to influence my subconscious mind with a strong 'f*ck it, I can do it' feeling, giving it powerful directions. I didn't have time for stop-start momentum and indecision. I needed to be clear, accurate and to the point. I needed laser-sharp focus and that was the end of that. I had decided. I had made an emphatic, f*ck it decision. I was going to be the master of my mind. I left no room for doubt.

My subconscious mind, in alignment with Source Energy, holds all knowledge and this means that I have access to a vast database. I was demanding access to it. I was clear and emphatic and in the present, as the subconscious mind only works in the present. I also trusted the process completely; there was no doubt. I felt, knew and believed that I would get inspiration, intuition and information.

Still with my hand on my heart I spoke to my inner child, tongue in cheek, but emphatically jostling her along. This is what I directed my mind to do:

O F*ck it – give me clarity on all the information I need for the publisher, before Monday, clearly, easily and accurately.

O F*ck it – give me clarity on the best information for the book quickly and easily. For my highest good and the highest good of all concerned, including the readers.

O *F*ck it* – I will retain all the information I need accurately in my mind. In my exam I will access accurately this information from the internal computer of my mind, quickly and easily.

I accurately directed my subconscious mind. Without a shred of doubt I released the outcome and saw my next client relaxed and aligned with Source Energy and trusting the process.

I had left no room for doubt and I created what I set out to do. It is worth noting that I did a lot of meditation and directing my mind over those few days and saved myself many hours and much wasted anxiety. I direct my mind in alignment with Source Energy a lot during the day, especially when I am at my busiest. As I've said, it is a fallacy that we do not have time to meditate; in fact, we do not have time not to meditate. The more I practise this, the better I am at it. This makes it very easy to trust the process. I know it works because I have proved it to myself. You will too.

Remember my mantra: 'just keep stepping, just keep stepping'. Well, I would like you to make your own *f*ck it* decisions and 'keep stepping' in your own life. One positively aligned decision – and step – after another will generate positive momentum, getting you to where you want to be. This is what Andrew did over a period of time.

ANDREW

Coming out was a major *f*ck it* decision in honouring Andrew's personal purpose in this life. If he had not made this decision, everything in his life would have been built on a lie. Going back to my computer metaphor, this was the upgraded version of Andrew. His connection with Source Energy was clearer and faster because he released resistance to his sexuality. This allowed momentum to gain and his personal 'inner light' was growing brighter and brighter. He made deliberate decisions around positive momentum and this gathered to such a degree around him he began to step into his higher purpose in this life.

In Andrew's sessions with me, I was preparing him to be able to step into this higher purpose in life, which involved the referendum. There was no room left for fear. In order to do this work and shine a light on equality, he needed to be fully aligned and standing in his own personal power. Remember, Andrew and his colleagues were holding a space for Ireland. That was no mean feat and it required a lot of energy. On the retreat in Bali, Andrew expected to delete any outdated files from his past. He was mindful that before he did anything else with the referendum, he needed to do this. In doing the inner work with his fearful child he released anything that was holding him back and allowed Source Energy to flow, uninterrupted, through him. This is the key to deliberately creating your own reality. No matter what you are trying to achieve, you have to release the resistance.

By the time I got to Bali that was the final piece of this particular puzzle. For years I had suffered from panic attacks. I had buried stuff deep. I remember with the panic attacks a terrible retching where nothing would ever come up. In my twenties I used to do it every day in the shower, and some days I ended up on my knees retching. Through my acupuncture sessions I had released a lot of that deep-rooted pain. It was brilliant. Over the years I had tolerated such abuse and bullying and I had buried it. During these sessions it started to come up and out of me.

In Bali one of the biggest things for me with regard to Source Energy was breath work. During a breath work session, I was lying down on the ground feeling tingly and then giddy. It was like all these emotions were coming up, and then in the next minute I threw myself up and I was violently sick. I can only describe it as belching noises coming out of me. They had to get a bucket and I proceeded to produce this disgusting stuff out of me. It was black, gooey and gross and that was it. That was another one of those feelings I got when I was in Bali. That was like 'that's done now' and relief.

In my practice I have helped others through a similar process. I can only explain it as a release of deep-rooted abuse. This experience is the exception rather than the norm, but these are some of the real fears that are lying within us. These are what hold us back from going forward. That inner child who is dragging, kicking and screaming at the leg of your trousers needs to be acknowledged and comforted. We all hold painful memories and fears, some of us more than others.

Without Andrew making many f*ck it decisions to release resistance within his life, he simply would not have been able to move forward. By making these decisions, by stepping little by little, gently working with his inner child, over time he was able to release his resistance.

KELLIE

Kellie's strong belief in her intuition meant that she expected something better to happen. She actually could hardly believe that the accident had happened at all. She had suffered a very big shock and shock is one of the main reasons we make f*ck it decisions. Another main reason for making f*ck it decisions is exasperation and desperation.

Much like Andrew and me, Kellie was moving through her situation in semi-awareness. The more she stepped through it, the more aware she became. This is the beauty of becoming a deliberate creator – the more you practise, the better you get at it.

Kellie made some huge *f*ck it* decisions. These decisions were directing her subconscious mind. She was putting her life back together again. Her *f*ck it* decisions had a major effect on her subconscious mind. She was giving her subconscious clear and unequivocal instructions with huge feeling. Therefore her subconscious had no choice but to obey. Kellie took time to:

O align with Source Energy,

O pull all her energy in and keep it to her close circle of family and friends,

O use all the tools in her toolbox,

O stay on the balcony and observe what kind of momentum she was creating,

O mindfully keep stepping,

O release resistance; acknowledge and comfort her inner very fearful child,

O not run away,

O make clear *f*ck it* decisions with feeling,

O expect to stay in the positive.

Here is a list of *f*ck it* decisions and expectations Kellie made:

O *F*ck it* – I just want to be healed and I expect this will happen.

O *F*ck it* – I am releasing resistance about taking the time to heal myself.

O *F*ck it* – I acknowledge the accident did happen to me and I expect to release the trauma.

O *F*ck it* – I am going to step through it to the end, it is a matter of principle.

O *F*ck it* – I am vulnerable, and that's okay, but I expect not to be so vulnerable very soon.

O *F*ck it* – I am working through a lot of stuff, but it will be over soon.

O *F*ck it* – I am not resisting it. I expect to look after my inner child.

O *F*ck it* – I will direct the manner in which I step through this court case.

O *F*ck it* – I will be comfortable with the uncomfortable.

Perhaps one of the best decisions she made, after deciding to stay and face her fears, was:

O *F*ck it* – I want to work in the music industry.

Kellie meant every single word of these decisions. She conjured up the feelings easily because she was pushed to her limits. The 'quick fix' would have been to run away. But she would have been dragging it all behind her, and it would have caught up with her eventually. The best and most effective solution was to decide to stand and mop it all up. This is always the best decision to make.

I love mantras, but they have to be meaningful to you. When you are changing big patterns, mantras keep you from jumping into the negative fearful chat in your head. Make no mistake, this is not just idle chit-chat, it is your conscious mind actively directing your subconscious all the time. When you find a mantra that suits you, you can substitute the negative jargon with something more positive. In this way you can be sure you are programming yourself to something better. Kellie shares a couple of her favourites:

When I was feeling absolutely rock bottom, my favourite one was 'the darkest hour is before the dawn'. I have a lot written down at home, but the other one I used was 'all is well', even though it wasn't well. I also read a lot of Wayne Dwyer,

Florence Shovel Shinn and Louise L. Hay. I was doing a lot of meditation. With
any process I find using the tools most important. Just getting up in the morning
and walking are great tools in themselves.

MEDITATION: THE SILVER CORD

Retreat to your comfort zone and sit easily with yourself for a few minutes. You are going to take this time to recharge your batteries and plug yourself into Source Energy. Through alignment with Source Energy your mind becomes tuned in, receiving downloads at will. Until now you have been comforting the fearful inner child and using this as a tool to reprogramme and delete outdated files. However, in this exercise you will be directing this inner child to pave the way in your life. You can also ask the child for clarity. Your inner child is a complete representation of your subconscious mind and all its different aspects. This meditation will help you restore balance and release any old, negative files.

Before you start, close your eyes and think of something you want clarity on. It could be how to heal your body, or how to bring more joy and happiness into your life. There may be a project you would like to bring to fruition; you may want to lose weight or make money. Whatever you are looking for clarity on, ask your inner child. Once you have set your intention, let it go and bring your attention inwards. Don't expect to receive clarity during the visualisation. Instead enjoy connecting with Source Energy and energising your system.

Settle down and just for these few minutes listen to the ebb and flow of your beautiful breath. Ebbing and flowing, ebbing and flowing, ebbing and flowing ...

In your mind's eye, visualise the universe and get a feel for every living thing in the universe. Imagine the planets and the moons that orbit them. Then gently bring your attention to planet earth and its vast oceans, forests and plains. Softly focus on the animals of the earth and all the human beings that inhabit this wonderful planet. Bring your awareness to yourself and from this higher perspective imagine being surrounded by a pulsing mass of vibrant silver energy. This is Source Energy and it is transcendent. It is limitless, pure potential and infinite intelligence; it is also fully present within each and every one of us. It is in all that exists. Now visualise strings of silver cords emanating from this energetic power house, feeding into each living thing on earth. These cords are similar to flexes of energy connecting you to Source Energy through your crown chakra.

Bring your attention to your crown chakra. See this chakra slowly start to open, spiralling in a clockwise motion. Imagine one of these silver energy cords connecting with your crown chakra. This pulsing energy awakens you from sleep mode, sending currents streaming through your astral body and on through your physical and emotional body. This is your very own power supply connecting you to the vast energetic intelligence.

As this download of energy takes place, it opens the crown chakra, illuminating the pituitary, pineal and hypothalamus glands, sending vibrant energy to your brain and your whole nervous system while it aligns your mind with the one-mind of Source Energy. It is at this point where the divine and human meet, where the transcendent and immanent energy mingle and become one. You begin to allow yourself to be immersed in this stream of blissful silver energy. Bathing in this infinite, crystalline, conscious awareness, you clearly direct your subconscious to release any negative outdated files it may have stored in the vast computer of your mind. Visualise sparks of silver energy minimising and zapping these old files.

Feel this crystal clear silver energy move towards your third eye. This is between your eyebrows at the centre of your forehead. The pulsating silver energy gently opens your third eye and it starts to spiral in a clockwise motion. Again, release anything blocking your way. See this electrical current of silver energy defusing any resistance you have to trusting your intuition and inner wisdom.

The energy from this radiant silver cord is now running parallel to your spinal cord. As it flows through your throat chakra it distributes vital energy, releasing creative blocks and igniting your creative abilities. This allows your voice to be heard and creates momentum around your confidence.

This energy starts to spark and ignite every cell in your body. You feel tingling sensations in your spine, hands and feet. Gaining momentum, this silver mass of charged energy travels down through your heart, illuminating, rebooting and revitalising every chamber of your heart. This is the centre of your being. See your heart being fully charged and expanded. Feel this expansion and breathe it in. Release any files of anger or resentment; see this energy fizz and dissolve any resistance into nothingness. Your heart acts as a conduit circulating energy to every cell and organ in your body.

This stream of energy continues through your solar plexus, which lies above your navel, and which is associated with your personal power. As the silver stream of positive energy fills this area you release any feelings of lack of self-worth. Filling this chakra with Source Energy allows you to increase positive momentum in all aspects of your life, releasing shame. This chakra feeds into your digestive system.

The silver pulsing energy moves on down toward your sacral chakra, below your navel. Fine threads of silver energy branch out into your reproductive system, clearing any blocks. Mentally release and let go of any negative feelings you have stored about your body or your sexuality. Take this opportunity to bring this crystal clear silver energy to any negative emotion you have stored and have created momentum around.

As this energy courses down through your root chakra at the base of the spine, it feeds into your sense of security and how you see yourself in this world. Filling this chakra with plenty of silver energy creates a solid foundation for you. Allowing this energy to penetrate your physical and astral body will ground you in the earth.

The silver cord acts like a root, branching out further and further through the earth's layers. You are now fully connected to Source Energy and grounded in the earth. You are perfectly aligned, re-energised and rebooted. You have released outdated limiting programming. Streams of consciousness have updated and upgraded you mentally, emotionally and physically. All negative tabs on your mental computer system have been closed down or minimised. This leads to a faster connection with Source Energy. Connecting with the one-mind enables us to compute as fast as we like with no limitations, no glitches.

You have made a clear decision to upgrade your system every day, increasing the speed at which you receive information. You are porous, receiving this energy from the main terminal, which is Source Energy.

See not only with your physical eyes but with your inner mind's eye. See this flow of energy dissolving all blocks and resistances. Feel and know that this flow of energy courses through every cell in your body, healing you. Open your ears to physically hear, but also listen to your body, your thoughts and words; this inner listening will give you vital information about negative patterns you need to change. Breathe Source Energy in through your nose and breathe all negativity out through your mouth. Now gently move your hands and feet and slowly bring yourself back to your comfort zone and to the outer world.

TOOLBOX

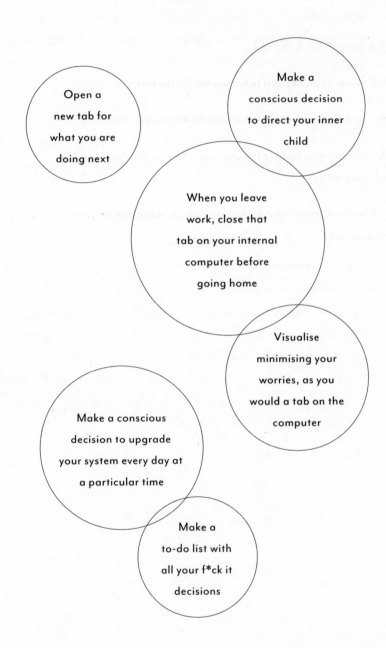

Open a new tab for what you are doing next

Make a conscious decision to direct your inner child

When you leave work, close that tab on your internal computer before going home

Visualise minimising your worries, as you would a tab on the computer

Make a conscious decision to upgrade your system every day at a particular time

Make a to-do list with all your f*ck it decisions

DIARY PAGES

1 Ask yourself the questions ...

*F*ck it* – have you decided to be healthy for the rest of your life?

*F*ck it* – have you decided to be wealthy for the rest of your life?

*F*ck it* – have you decided to live the rest of your life through joy and happiness?

2 Write down what *f*ck it* decisions you have made around your three desires.

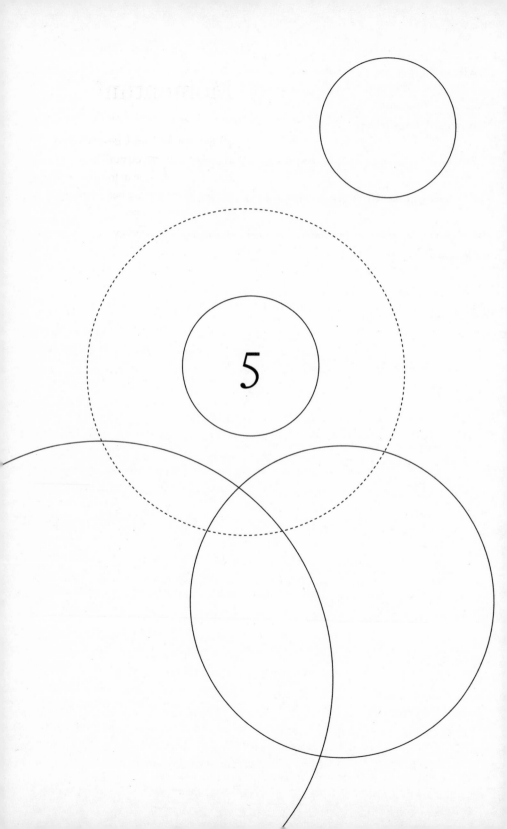

5

Momentum

'Things flow and are indirectly linked
together ... and if you push here,
something will move at the other end of
the world. If you strike here, something,
somewhere will wince.'

FYODOR DOSTOYEVSKY

Tuning in

THE SOLAR PLEXUS CHAKRA

Before we go any further, put your hand on your heart and connect with your inner child. Rub your heart chakra and tell your little child that you are with her. Inwardly say to her, 'Do you know what? You are great and I love you.' Really feel for your inner child as you would feel for a small child in your life. Even this small action integrates your fearful child, aligning her with your growth and what you are achieving as you read this book. Now close your eyes and gently place soft focus on your solar plexus chakra, the area above your navel. The purpose of this chakra is transformation, activity and power. In your mind's eye visualise the colour yellow and listen to the ebb and flow of your breath. Ebbing and flowing, ebbing and flowing, ebbing and flowing ...

What you will learn from this chapter

—

Be in awareness of what you are doing. You are now beginning to give your subconscious mind clear instruction. This is necessary for deliberately creating. You are gently focusing in. In this chapter I will be explaining about momentum. Everything is possible with momentum and nothing is possible without it, so it is integral to creation. I will be exploring positive and negative momentum, conscious and unconscious momentum, and indecisive 'stop-start' momentum.

I will be using the rollercoaster concept as a way of impressing momentum on your mind. We will be exploring different ways of using momentum through the example of how to create a lover. We will be tuning in and accessing the field of pure potential. The practice of tantra is the intertwining of the spiritual and physical; where the divine and human meet. Together we will delve into consummating and conceiving ideas, using the metaphor of the embryonic idea. There will be some more lovely tools for your ever-expanding toolbox and, of course, stories from Andrew, Kellie and me. The visualisation for this chapter is all about accessing the field of pure potential at will. As always, your diary pages at the end of this chapter are your sanctuary as they are the magic space for you to explore what type of momentum you are creating in your life. This is very important.

What is momentum?

—

Imagine you are heading off to a funfair on a cold day at Christmas. You are particularly interested in going on the rollercoaster. Uncomfortably strapped in and feeling very nervous, you wait for the ride to begin.

You start to focus inwardly, mentally psyching yourself up. Your subconscious is being triggered by memories of rollercoaster rides from your childhood. These memories were stored in your subconscious computer and have been regenerated. Alarm bells start to go off in your head, and you question whether you really want to do this to yourself. The warning signals ripple through your body, your hands begin to sweat and you're getting that churning feeling in your stomach. Your inner child is on high alert and is ready to leg it. But you coax her into staying put, in complete trepidation about what is to come.

Initially the rollercoaster is in a state of rest or inertia. As it starts off there is very little momentum. It's going so slowly, in fact, that you wonder whether it's moving at all. Gradually there is a small increase in speed, but nonetheless the momentum is gathering. As the direction of the ride changes and it starts to hurtle down slopes and around curves there is a large acceleration in speed. Momentum has gathered, and the ride is in full swing. It is this type of momentum that allows the ride to achieve the loop the loop traditionally associated with rollercoasters.

Anything that is in motion has momentum. It has a beginning and then it slowly builds up force and speed, expanding and gathering all the time. This includes your thoughts, words and deeds.

You are generating many different types of momentum with your creations all the time. For instance, you can create positive and negative momentum around what you create, or around indecision. There is a very high chance that you are creating a lot of negative momentum unconsciously, and this has become automatic.

It is very important to recognise what kind of momentum you are creating. Remember, if you plant a potato you will grow and harvest potatoes.

Equally, if you create negative momentum, and feed this negative momentum, it will grow and you will harvest the fruits of your labours. Just like the rollercoaster in motion, momentum will gather around whatever you plant. The universe doesn't mind what momentum you create. Momentum is momentum. The universe also leaves it to you to figure it all out. However, it is you who has to live out what you create and sometimes we can create our own hell on earth. This is why I try to make sure I am in awareness of just what kind of momentum I am creating.

Unconsciously creating momentum

—

In general we create momentum obliviously. We block ourselves with conditioning and fear. This is our inner child holding us back, resisting the way ahead. We move forwards in our lives, then we hold ourselves back, we struggle and then start stepping, we get gripped by fear and stop again. We go around in the same loop the loop, like a rollercoaster. Time after time we block the flow of positive momentum in our lives. Instead, we end up building far more momentum around negativity or indecision. This is what I call stop-start momentum.

Below I have created an exercise that will show you how to create momentum with soft focus, decisions, releasing resistance and intense focus. You will be working closely with your inner child. This little one is the perfect tool in helping you to create momentum and in establishing new neural pathways in your mind.

An exercise in momentum

—

In this exercise I want you to imagine that you would really love to be in a relationship with your soulmate – or at least someone you can have a bit of fun with. You have had your heart broken in a previous relationship and you have started to become a bit of a recluse. You have now decided to entertain the idea of a partner for a few seconds. This feels relatively good. But the thought of exposing yourself on an online dating site curdles your blood and nearly gives you apoplexy. You flatly refuse to entertain the idea. Welcome to what I call the inertia stage. There is absolutely no momentum around dating and never will be as long as you remain in this state.

Now let's stand on the balcony and see just what type of momentum you have created here. For a few moments you were more aligned with Source Energy and had opened yourself up to the field of pure potential. The thought popped into your head and was conceived, becoming a particle of reality deep within you. Applying soft focus for a few seconds allowed you to feel and believe that you could find a partner. The spark of positive momentum was ignited. Your creation was on its way. However, your subconscious mind was triggered by the thoughts of past rejection and your inner child started to have a meltdown.

Your previous experience of a broken heart was enough for this child to put up every barrier and block known to man. In unawareness of what was going on, you completely conceded to the fears of the little one. Now she is running the show, driving the runaway car. She is directing your love life from negative memories, and not from what's actually happening in this present moment. Your fearful inner child, not your adult self, has made the decision to shut down. This present moment

'Now let's stand on the balcony and see what type of
momentum you have created ...'

holds potential but you have now blocked the momentum necessary to propel you into positive action.

So now let's fast forward – it could be ten minutes or ten years into the future. You realise you need to create some momentum around the situation. At this point you have three choices.

CHOICE NO. 1
CREATING MOMENTUM IN UNAWARENESS AND NEGATIVITY

You look in the mirror and sigh. Turning sideways, you critically assess your slightly protruding belly. You are softly focusing on all the negatives. You are in complete unawareness of what you are creating in the bigger picture of your life. Picking up a dress, you fling it on the bed, 'That has short sleeves and I can't wear it – my arms are too big.' The resistance is gathering momentum. Then you cast your eyes on your face and have a good rant at how you look. Your anxiety and disgust gain further momentum. The speed increases and you vehemently start verbally abusing your inner child, again in complete unawareness of the consequences of your actions. 'Who would be bothered with me anyway? I'm overweight and my hair is awful.' Imagine a beautiful child standing in front of you. Instead of highlighting the child's wonderful aspects, you rip the child to shreds, stripping the child of all confidence and self-worth, mindlessly bashing and bruising this poor child. That kind of abuse demolishes a person's self-esteem and causes serious damage.

This is negative momentum in unawareness and it is rapidly gaining speed. You add more fuel to your fire and, running a hundred steps ahead of yourself, start to think of sex. You haven't even got a date, never mind spoken to this fictional partner. Now god forbid there should be a sexual encounter; you would probably have to take off your clothes! Well, that's enough to push you over the edge. At this point the momentum is hurtling along not unlike the rollercoaster. The speed and force of your thoughts are propelling this imaginary date into disaster. You are now applying intense focus and you are creating a lot of anxiety. You feel overwhelmed and disgusted with yourself. What your subconscious feels, it believes, and you are conjuring up mighty negative feelings.

The rollercoaster is about to come off the rails. You have successfully conjured up feelings of disgust and self-loathing, along with a myriad of other negative feelings that will play themselves out in all sorts of ways in your outer life. Well done – you have successfully created your own reality. However, this is in unawareness and negativity and it is my guess this is not your true intention.

Then you start to think, 'You know what? I like being on my own. All those dating sites are no good anyway,' and you talk yourself into believing that you would never find anyone decent on them. Deciding to put the whole idea to bed, without the partner, you close yourself down and block yourself off.

Now let's stand on the balcony and see just what type of momentum you have created – as if you don't already know.

You had started to think about dating, opening the door into the field of pure potential and peeking in. Finding a lover is a possibility if you would only let momentum gather. Your subconscious, also known as your inner child, was triggered by a very fearful situation. You had been hurt in the past by one or more lovers, and it is this memory that is sending your inner child into trauma. Not only does your inner child feel threatened by a lover, but it also goes back much further, bringing up other feelings, which might stem from your childhood, lack of self-worth being one of them. These feelings are now added to the pot. Initially you had placed soft negative focus on your lack of self-worth, but as momentum gains you put intense focus on it, to such a degree that you decide to shut yourself off entirely. This is all done in unawareness, and you then look outward and blame the dating sites or anything that will deflect from your frightened inner child.

CHOICE NO. 2
CREATING MOMENTUM AROUND INDECISION

We all tend to be indecisive, but the more indecisive you are, the worse things will be. You may save yourself from bad decisions, but you also keep yourself from the good ones too. Instead you are creating a loop and become trapped in perpetual indecision. This is where stop-start momentum comes into play. You want to go out on a date, you may even have the outfit, but procrastination keeps you from moving forward. Procrastination is fear. Unfortunately, your inner child is being triggered and you don't know what to do. You're swinging from, 'Yes, I want to bring someone into my life', to 'Oh no, I couldn't possibly do that', then launching into all the negative scenarios mentioned above.

This is like planting a seed in the ground, immediately digging it up again, but still expecting the seed to grow, and you are doing it over and over again. There is very little soft focus, no decisions, no releasing resistance and no intense focus. The only thing that is being created here is indecision, again and again.

When you stand on the balcony to see just what type of momentum you have created, you see it is only momentum around indecision and nothing else.

CHOICE NO. 3
CREATING MOMENTUM IN AWARENESS AND POSITIVITY

Let's go back to the first choice and pick up where we left off. You have had your fill of inner child-bashing. Your intuition is telling you that it is getting you nowhere, and exasperation has taken over. You really want a partner. In deciding not to let fear stand in your way and block you from going forwards, you take a leap of faith. This ceases the intense focus you have put on negative momentum. You are taking your focus away from the negative and softly focusing on the positive. The blazing fire of negativity is beginning to weaken. Following your intuition tentatively, you are starting to put into practice all you are learning. You have decided to go online to look for a suitable date and your inner child is hysterical. However, you are now kindling a fire of positivity.

Instead of ignoring your inner child, you mindfully acknowledge her fear. It is apparent to you that ignoring your inner child only keeps you caught in negative momentum. You resolve to re-parent her instead. Slowly you begin to become aware of her deep-rooted issues around self-worth and relationships. It begins to dawn on you that this is what has kept you blocked all these years. This is your intuition guiding you. These self-worth issues have never been recognised. It is this resistance that is stopping you having a new relationship. You start to take responsibility for your inner child. By working with your intuition and inner child you are actively increasing momentum around bringing a lover into your life.

Feeling you could meditate, you make up your mind to use this as a tool to open yourself up to the field of pure potential. In trusting the process, without much of a guarantee that it works, you begin to align yourself with Source Energy. You are making room to bring someone new into your life. You are taking the first few steps in releasing resistance. Remember, the ripples always move from the inside out. Getting yourself aligned is the key to finding the right partner. Before your meditation, simply ask your inner child to let go of any fear. In slowly healing and letting go of your self-worth and relationship issues, you align with who you really are. This big person within you is confident, strong, loving and open.

If you are not aligned with the real you, you are tuned into your fearful inner child instead. This child will display itself outwardly as closed, fearful and lacking in confidence. You are allowing your inner child to form your intimate relationships. This will only attract another child, someone with a similar disposition who hasn't aligned themselves, and is tuned into their own fearful inner child. If you want to attract someone who is aligned, align yourself first.

Spiritual re-parenting
—

Along with meditation, one of the best tools you have is the capacity to re-parent your inner child. When fearful feelings come up, this is your child calling you. Don't run away from her. Acknowledge her feelings. Tell your inner child that you are moving forward. Make sure she knows she will be your priority; you will be looking after her first, every step of the way. You are conjuring up feelings of security, love and self-worth, or whatever feeling is appropriate to what you want to create. When you actively reprogramme your subconscious mind in a positive way, the momentum builds around your desire. By focusing in on the child you are also placing soft focus on what you want to create. This will not only serve you with this particular issue, but it will affect every aspect of your life. It's a domino effect. Change one thing toward the positive and everything changes toward the positive.

Mantra

—

The use of a mantra helps you to re-wire yourself. In creating new neural pathways, it is probably best to focus on one desire at a time. You don't want to confuse yourself. Before you go to sleep at night is an ideal time to comfort your inner child and soothe her into a new pattern. At this period between wakefulness and sleep, your brain waves slow down into an alpha state, allowing freer access to the subconscious. This re-wiring process requires tools, so metaphors and mantras are ideal in helping you to do this. A mantra could be something as simple as 'I *am* good enough.' This can be very powerful if said with feeling to your inner child. Another simple but powerful mantra is, 'I can do this', progressing to 'I am doing this' as the momentum increases and you get stronger in your conviction, feeling and knowing.

Talk to your child. Tell her that you really are worthy of being loved and tell her you love her. Become very comfortable with this little inner child. You are actively creating a shift and your imagination, visualisations and mantras are excellent tools to help you create positive momentum. It is very important to slowly make sure you feel what you are telling the child. Keep in mind that the subconscious doesn't listen to what you are saying, it feels.

Cast your mind back to the examples of creating negative momentum around manifesting a partner. You have built up this momentum to such a degree that you feel the results of the negative chatter within you. You feel anxious and fearful, and your body reacts to this – you might even get a sick feeling in the pit of your stomach. This is because your subconscious really believes these feelings. You have successfully conjured up and created a feeling. But it is negative.

When talking to your inner child, it is not good enough to recite mantras off the top of your head without really feeling what you are saying. If you can conjure up negative feelings in unawareness and get a negative result, you can conjure up positive ones in awareness and get a positive result. Reach inside yourself and imagine this lovely little girl within you. She is real and in distress, and she needs you to comfort and acknowledge her. If you had a pet name as a child, you can use that. My grandfather used to call me 'chicken', so when I am mindfully programming my subconscious mind and catch myself conjuring up negative chatter or feel any negativity within me at all, I put my hand on my heart and say: 'Ah chicken, I know you are afraid, but I am here, I will mind you, you are safe.' When you find yourself breaking into negative momentum with regard to self-worth or fear on any level, be very kind to the inner child, and gently coax her back. Emphasise all her good points and minimise any negative ones. Get to know her and love her. Listen out for the chatter in your mind and when you catch her going into negativity, talk her out of it. Gradually, by keeping yourself aligned with Source Energy, you keep yourself open to infinite intelligence and the field of pure potential.

Keep stepping

—

As you progress with your dating project (or any other desire), it is important to keep your inner child under your wing and also make room because your inner teenager might want to show up. Especially throughout the first date; it is here she will need you the most. Gradually step her through the first kisses and sexual encounters. Always stay true and honour who you really are and how you feel. You don't want to create any more negative memories for the inner child to get upset about. Throughout the process, try to maintain conscious awareness in resetting the vast computer that is your subconscious mind. The subconscious mind needs to be acknowledged. It loves repetition, feeling, knowing, and it requires direction. So the constant comforting is an ideal way to meet all your subconscious requirements.

Studies have shown that it can take an average of 66 days to create new neural pathways in the brain. This is very achievable by staying aligned with Source Energy. You can amplify this energy by conjuring up positive feelings and knowings instead of negative ones. Then actively re-parent your inner child. This will create copious amounts of positive momentum. This is deliberately creating your own reality and it takes practice before it starts to become an automatic response.

Get into the driving seat

—

You are changing your life and that takes a little bit of time and patience. Keep in mind that it is a process. It is a lot like learning to drive a car or ride a bike. It can be difficult to pay attention to everything. It can even be a little mentally exhausting at first. When you are learning to drive, you turn off the radio in the car and focus on the task at hand; you simply don't have enough mental space to learn to drive and listen to the radio at the same time. That is because you are consciously working hard, consciously directing and programming your subconscious mind. When you have had a few lessons and are becoming more competent, all the processes of driving or riding a bike become automatic; you are on automatic pilot. This frees your conscious mind to attend to other things.

'The conscious mind may be compared to a fountain playing in the sun and falling back into the great subterranean pool of subconscious from which it rises.'

SIGMUND FREUD

This is similar to what you are doing with all these processes in this book. It may be difficult to remember everything. You might still doubt what you are doing and think it is a lot of nonsense, and that's okay. But with a bit of perseverance, practice and trust, this will become your automatic response. You are shifting your awareness and that is a mighty leap. You are moving into a conscious state of awareness and stepping into the field of pure potential. That is commendable, so be proud of yourself, even if it's difficult at first.

You are really getting to work now on developing your intimate relationship with Source Energy and the field of pure potential.

Source Energy is rich and fertile, flowing endlessly with potential. Source Energy needs to express itself through you. You are a conduit or a pathway for this infinite intelligence to reveal itself to the world. How else would Source Energy be seen? But you are not merely a channel for this wonderful energy. You are a co-creator. You are in symbiotic union with Source Energy, much like when you were in your mother's womb. You are a reflection of Source Energy made physical.

To co-create with Source Energy means creating momentum and intimacy with this energy. When you consummate your relationship, it allows you create enough momentum to conceive ideas from the field of pure potential. Otherwise what you wish to create cannot be conceived and you block yourself off from your desires.

Remember:

O All of what you wish to co-create is in the field of pure potential.

O The field of pure potential is pure consciousness, limitless and boundless abundance.

O You are an integral part of this field; you cannot remove yourself from it. However, you can decide to close yourself off from it.

You have free choice. Closing yourself off means relying on your own rather limited ability. This chokes off all your desires. There can be nothing gained from separating yourself from unconditional love, power and strength. Restricting your abundance serves no purpose. This type of self-sabotage alienates you, and feeling alienated leads to insecurity and conflict. Inner conflict is a sure sign of not being aligned.

O Constant access to the field of pure potential can be maintained through alignment.

O The field of pure potential is where the divine and human meet and co-create.

O Co-creating with Source Energy means that there are no limits – everything is possible.

It is very hard, if not impossible, to comprehend the limitlessness of Source Energy. During meditation you align yourself to this energy. I often think it's like getting under the shower. Every single part of you gets under the shower and you align yourself with the shower head. You don't leave your head or an arm or leg outside the shower. You are fully aligned with it. Then you can feel the water raining down on you.

O During meditation all your chakras open, you are porous, everything flows.

O You are in a state of allowing.

The embryonic concept
—

The practice of tantra is an intertwining of the spiritual and the physical. This is the sacred space where the divine and human meet. The purpose is to become one. It is here that conception of your wishes and desires can take place. When the spark of your desire enters your mind, it is conceived instantly. It becomes the smallest speck of possibility. The first signs of momentum begin. Your wishes have now become like embryos in the womb of your mind.

The seed of possibility has the capacity to form and grow like the embryo in the womb of your mind. This seed of possibility will eventually be born into life as we know it. If you can't connect, think and feel this seed of possibility, you can't have it. All human life, all of creation and all of what you wish to create in your life is the direct result of this divine energetic union.

But how do I bring my desires from the field of pure potential to the field in my back yard? Let's play and have fun with your inner child ...

Your subconscious feels, absorbs and loves symbols and images; it is like a sponge. To help create momentum, let me give your inner child a metaphor that she will enjoy. Your child will then be able to refer to this metaphor as a way to create what you desire. This is a tool to access the field of pure potential, knowing how to deliberately create your own reality from the conception of an idea, to the gestation and finally into the birthing of the idea. None of this would be possible without momentum.

The creative process
—

O During the first trimester your idea/desire is conceived by aligning with Source Energy. Meditation is the big tool to use in this part of the process.

O During the second trimester your idea/desire is nurtured within the womb of your mind. Your inner child practice is a big tool to use at this part of the process.

O During the third trimester your idea/desire is gaining momentum. You prepare for birth by releasing resistance. Your big tools here are your inner child practice and meditation.

At the early stages of conceiving an idea, it is a flicker of reality:

O The momentum around it isn't very strong.

O It seems as if the idea is 'just there'.

O But your doubts and fears sabotage your trust in this.

For example, the idea to buy a house has been conceived. You can feel it as a lovely possibility in the recesses of the womb of your mind. You sense and know it would be the right thing to do. Your intuition is pointing you in the right direction. But immediately you resist it with fear. How in the name of goodness would you be able to afford it? Who do you think you are? How are you going to do it? And on it goes. This constant barrage of negativity is your conditioning, emanating from your subconscious mind.

O This is fear and this is your inner child calling you.

O Your self-doubt is also based on your present circumstances, and what you have already created.

O This is old news, but if you pay too much attention to it, it will remain ongoing news.

You are now creating negative momentum around your tiny embryonic idea, so how is it supposed to grow?

What you need to do is nurture this embryonic idea at the early stages. Your desire is vulnerable and has not formed enough to give you any clarity. Metaphorically speaking, you cannot see what colour eyes and hair the baby has; your idea needs soft focus and allowing, as it is forming deep in the chasms of your mind. Momentum is growing slowly. You can nurture your desire by meditating and being careful who you discuss your idea with. The idea is percolating.

ROAD BLOCKS TO YOUR CREATIONS

We put up resistance in all sorts of ways. You can be very sceptical and you can't see how your idea is going to form. For the life of you, you cannot see how it will be achieved. You may be concerned with how you will get the money to realise your idea. Or, for example, how you will create a business and get people to invest in you. However, if you were pregnant and creating a baby, you wouldn't worry about how the heart or lungs are formed. You can't see how the supreme creation of a baby will be achieved but you take it for granted that it will.

However, you will quite often dismiss the idea forming in the womb of your mind by paying more attention to your external situation rather than allowing time for momentum to gather around your idea. You will try to block and resist momentum. This is your inner child and she needs you to help her move forwards. Remember, you are often changing deeply held learned behavioural, societal and generational patterns. You are out of your comfort zone and this child is throwing a wobbly. It is precisely at this point you start to put into action all that you have learned about your inner child and her needs. Get out your toolbox and apply your tools.

The funny thing is, it is much easier to create a million euro than it is to create a heart or spinal cord. Yet women all around the world manage to do this every day of the week and nobody bats an eyelid. People don't know how their bodies work to form the intricate organs, glands, muscles and bones of a baby. But they innately trust the process.

BACK ON TRACK

When you have conceived an idea and it is something that your intuition is keen on, allow the idea time to form in the womb of your mind. It is creating momentum but it is still weak. Don't speak about your idea to others, just in case they put you off. Feel around your idea, and don't pay any heed yet to your outer circumstances. I often say to myself when I have a really good idea, 'I don't know how I'm going to do this yet, but I will.' I am giving myself permission to believe I can and I say it with conviction. One of my favourite mantras is 'I can do this'. As my idea progresses I change this mantra to 'I am doing this'. Don't just say the mantra in unawareness. Say it with conviction – 'I *can* do this' – create a feeling around it. I am taking my inner child by the hand and gently leading her to the idea, encouraging her to feel that she can do whatever she wants to do. This child of mine isn't stupid and there is no fooling her. If I only pay her lip service and I do not present myself to her with courage and conviction she simply will not believe me. If my parenting of the child is without substance, she will still be afraid and resist me.

Continue to conjure up momentum around positive feelings about your idea and don't feed the negative feelings. Don't ignore the negatives either, just comfort your inner child until you bring her to the point where she can start to feel and know this idea is possible. Continue to ignore your external circumstances. Do not feed doubt. Meditate each day, as much as you can. After each meditation, ask for guidance around your idea. Do the little things on the circumferences of your desire; this will support and nurture it. You are creating internal momentum and soft focus. This is where everything starts.

Momentum builds little by little over time. Just like the cells of the embryo, momentum gradually builds as a result of many things gathering together. This activity amasses and multiplies and eventually becomes powerful, accumulating and building on itself. Ultimately momentum takes on a life of its own just as in the development of a baby. Momentum is momentum; no matter what you want to create, it is the same principle.

JUDITH

I want to tell you about how I created momentum around this book. It was 1987. Before I went to work in the airline business, I did a brief computer course in Ely House, near Baggot Street, in the heart of Dublin City. I always arrived too early in the morning, so I would go for breakfast in a little café not far from Ely House. I was 18 at the time and used to sit with my little notebook, people-watching, and I would write. I would write about the people I saw in the café. I am an empath and have a natural ability to feel and perceive others intuitively. I have been doing this since I was a child. All my life I have relied heavily on my heightened sense of intuition. As a result, when I meet people, I automatically tune in to their energy. So there I was with nothing better to do but tune in to other people and write it all down.

It was here I decided to write my book. I decided I wanted to be a writer and I had opened myself to the field of pure potential. It was a happy time in my life and I was very aligned with Source Energy. The idea was conceived. The spark of momentum had begun. How and when the idea was going to be born, I had no idea. I did not know the form it was going to take, the topic I was going to write about or how I would even get it published. All I can tell you is the story of how it has unfolded and gained momentum over 31 years. But let me briefly trace it for you. Sometimes our creations have a very slow gestation period; other things can come instantaneously. This is due to many factors. When an idea is conceived it will come in to this reality when you are ready, when you have released all the resistance to it and fully aligned yourself with it.

At that period in my life I was fully aware of Source Energy, intuition, feeling, knowing, decisions and expectations. But it took me a 'couple' of years to acknowledge and honour my inner child. She also put up a hell of a lot of resistance to me exposing my true self. This was coupled with the fact that I was not too au fait with momentum, receiving or allowing. I had to figure those out and put them all together. I was writing this book, but I didn't consciously know it. Looking back on it now, I already had the first four chapters of the book but I was consciously unaware at that point. I was unaware that I was living out the chapters in my life, gathering the information for these pages over 31 years of living the content.

I never really mentioned the idea of my book to anyone. This allowed the embryonic idea to mass and grow slowly. I knew deep down that it was there. It was safely embedded in the lining of the womb of my mind. There is no time limit on your ideas, no sell-by date, and no age limit either. Age doesn't come into it. When you are ready and release resistance your desires come quickly; they just pop in and are borne out. It can be a very easy birth if you release resistance.

Over the years I wrote a lot. I often stood on the balcony of my life, trying to figure out what my inner fearful child was doing and why. Momentum had gathered just enough to allow me glimpses of the general topic. Source Energy, infinite intelligence, and the field of pure potential had been my obsession all my life in many different ways. I still didn't have the names for them, but I had the feeling and I built momentum around the feeling.

Now let me fast forward from 1987 through many exciting, action-packed, happy and at times heart-breaking years. It is now 2010, one of those years when you either sink or swim. As I mentioned earlier, 2010 saw me back in Dublin, all but broken on many levels, including financially. It was then I decided to make my alignment with Source Energy a priority. I was terrified. I just didn't have myself to consider, I had my three beautiful children too. My inner child was rooted to the spot with fear. I made the decision that instead of beating up my inner child, I would celebrate her. I had always put her last, now I made a decision to finally put her first. The ripples always move from the inside out, so I looked after her and made her strong again. I nurtured her, meditated and did a lot of walking. I finally decided to honour the sacred agreement I had with Source Energy and myself. No more running away from this; I was ready to release resistance and stand in my own power.

I sat down with a large flipchart and drew out all that I had in my head. Everything I felt within me, I emptied onto a large piece of paper. I still have it. I had conceived many ideas over the years in moments of alignment. A lot of them were safely tucked up in the womb of my mind, and now they were gaining enough momentum for me to get more clarity. I scribbled them down, sketching out what I wanted to do with my life. I had many empathetic talents, now how was I going to use them? I remembered my father saying to me years ago, 'If you knit, knit.' In other words, whatever you are good at, stick with it. I was really good with intuition, empathy, feeling and Source Energy. So I decided to stick to what I was good at.

I had written my entire practice on that page, along with talks, seminars and books, among other things. I didn't know how I was going to do any of it. Remember, my outer circumstances were reflecting that which I had already created, and my prospects looked exceedingly dismal. I was a divorced mother of three with no job in a recession. To compound matters, I was now thinking of starting my own business. But I ignored the seemingly dim future. I did what I had to do and kept stepping. My children were a massive influence on me. Every time I looked at them I was powerfully reminded that I was hugely abundant, and I used this to conjure abundance to make me feel rich.

I realised that almost everything I put on my big piece of paper in 2010 had been in the womb of my mind since 1987. I had begun my crusade to deliberately create my own reality, and now I was beginning to give birth to these ideas. I completed an honours degree in theology in a quest to understand Source Energy better. I even manifested two wonderful rooms in a building in the leafy suburbs of Dublin City. Ironically, the name of the building where I opened my practice is Ely House. There are no co-incidences in life. This book was conceived 31 years ago in Ely House in the heart of Dublin City and was laboured and birthed in another Ely House, this time in the suburbs of Dublin.

I had used myself as a case study in researching my books throughout the years. Nowadays I meditate a lot, direct my subconscious mind, look after my inner child and choose to create positive momentum in every aspect of my life.

Now we'll look at how Andrew and his colleagues used momentum during the marriage equality campaign. This will give you a great feeling for how to use momentum in all its different guises.

ANDREW

Andrew and all those people involved in the marriage equality campaign had been gathering momentum around it for years. But, just like the rollercoaster, what was the point when the momentum around the campaign became unstoppable?

Let me think. From my point of view the momentum really started to gather in 2013. In my opinion the government were basically fearful of calling a referendum on marriage equality, probably because they didn't want to lose votes. So they put it to the Constitutional Convention to decide whether to call a referendum or not. They came back to the government, and recommended overwhelmingly that yes ,the referendum should take place.

There is no doubt in my mind, the reason the Constitutional Convention voted yes was because of all the momentum created in the intervening years between 2008 and 2013. I remember back in 2008 we were laughed at by a lot of people in the gay community, because they never thought it would happen. Many gay people genuinely said to me, 'I never thought that marriage equality would happen in my lifetime.'

Personally, I felt the rights of a minority should never be voted on by a majority because the chances of a vote in favour of the minority are very slim. Therefore the campaign needed to open people up by changing old deep-seated patterns.

So when we started in 2008 we essentially became the storyteller. We got couples to tell their stories, and in doing so we began to change hearts and minds in the process. It was through these stories and by repeating the message over and over that the momentum slowly began. Marriage equality's core message of love and equality has always stayed the same. People's minds started to change and we got more and more supporters.

During the campaign we constantly reiterated the positive even though we encountered the negative a lot. We repeatedly instilled positivity in people, they in turn instilled it in others and the message spread.

I always remember having a session with you and learning about holding a space for people. I also recall learning the power of this in yoga training. I vividly remember talking to you about it and you said, 'You are holding space for Ireland.' During the campaign we didn't fully realise what marriage equality meant for people. This was not just LGBT people but a huge proportion of people in general wanted a better Ireland. It was only after the campaign that the vastness of the 'space held' became apparent. The referendum heralded in something new.

It was a departure from sexual suppression where the large majority of Irish people couldn't even talk about sex. It was cutting the ties of the repressive Ireland of old.

As we began to realise how much space we were holding, the momentum started to multiply. It increased so much, to the point that the momentum actually propelled us forward without fear. Then there was the moment of realisation when we said, 'We are doing this. Whether we win or lose we are about to do it. There is no going back.' The success of the campaign was because of all the momentum we created and because we had such belief in what we were doing.

Andrew recalls that the government were fearful of calling a referendum. Remember the fearful inner child? Well, when a group of us gather we can create en masse in the positive or in the negative. The marriage equality campaign was triggering the collective subconscious in Dáil Éireann. Unsurprisingly this was upsetting the inner-child fears of many of those involved.

> 'Out of the huts of
> history's shame
> I rise
> Up from a past that's
> rooted in pain
> I rise.'
> MAYA ANGELOU

By putting the referendum decision to the Constitutional Convention it could be said that the government handed over responsibility. The momentum at this point was stop-start. Fear en masse was restricting momentum from gathering. However, when the Constitutional Convention voted Yes, this was a different story. The fears were still there but the positive momentum the marriage equality campaign had mustered over the years suddenly gained speed. They were conjuring up the feeling of confidence. The rollercoaster ride was about to get into full swing.

When the go-ahead for the referendum was given, the campaign faced a greater obstacle. The collective fear they faced from the government was nothing compared to the concentrated fear they were going to face across Ireland. The marriage equality campaign reached into the subconscious mind of each and every adult in Ireland, and it was about to trigger huge fear. The collective inner child of Ireland was on the verge of erupting, bringing up monumental issues regarding, sex, repression, religion, equality and shame, and highlighting just how traumatised many Irish people were, and how as a nation we had suffered from generations of sexual repression and abuse.

The gay community were the abused. But they didn't turn into the abusers. Instead they soothed the inner child of Ireland. They used metaphors and stories. They spoke of love and equality. They touched hearts, conjuring up a sense of personal power, not only in the gay community but in Ireland as a whole. They aligned themselves with love and this is what eventually gained enormous momentum. 'We are doing this' became the collective mantra.

Andrew regularly visited me during the referendum to maintain his alignment. This ensured that he stayed on the balcony and kept the bigger picture in his line of vision. We were paving the way in awareness. Our conversations on holding a space for Ireland were extremely important: he could have become too bogged down in narrowly focusing on specifics. It was easier for me to stand on the balcony and look down, and what I saw was transformational for Ireland. Andrew stayed on the balcony with me. Ireland's paradigm shift was created through collective momentum. The Irish people crawled out of its sexually repressed past, shining a major light on equality, becoming a catalyst for change in the world.

KELLIE

Kellie's accident ignited negative momentum, and the fire was rapidly fuelled by the legal proceedings in Australia.

The other fire Kellie had burning was her post-traumatic stress. By now she had that once-raging fire pretty much under control. She had dampened the fire by staying aligned, using meditation, walking, her family support structure, her psychologist, physiotherapy and me. She knew that in time the fire would go out. All she had to do was continue to quench it with as much positivity as she could.

However, the court case was an inferno. But Kellie wasn't using her energy to resist the momentum that was gathering around it. She was aware that once momentum builds to that level it just has to play out, and resisting it is futile. Instead, she was containing it and not feeding it. All the time Kellie was staying aligned and on the balcony. She was cautiously being mindful not to fuel the fire with logs of negativity. Instead, she waited patiently and used her intuition to keep herself from getting burned by this Australian bush fire.

Here is an idea of what Kellie had to face during the time leading up to the court case.

KELLIE:

The insurance company employed detectives. They followed me, in Ireland, over a six-week period leading up to Christmas. Obviously I wasn't consciously aware this was happening. But on a deeper level my intuition was alerting me to something. I noticed that I started closing the driveway gates every day even if I was alone in the house. There was a feeling within me that I didn't feel safe. I was tuning into something but I didn't know what.

It was Christmas week when I found out I was being followed. This was a moment of devastation; I felt completely violated. I was horrified that my family and friends were exposed to this. I remember coming to you and saying, 'That's it, I am done.' I called my lawyer in Sydney and said 'I'm done, this is crazy.' Unfortunately that's how insurance companies work, and they were trying to scare me. To stay true to myself and continue was very hard to do.

JUDITH:

That was one of the reasons I wanted you to participate in this book. You were staying true to yourself against all the odds.

KELLIE:

To find that out when you are already struggling with a very difficult situation was very hard. I was doing physio all the time. Funnily enough, they never documented that. I was trying my best to heal after the accident. I was investing all my time into working on me. I spent a lot of my time here with you too.

JUDITH:

But that's precisely how you survived it, you kept yourself aligned. You came to me, you were walking, doing physio and using all your other tools. That is what propelled you forwards. You were creating positive momentum around all of that, and trying not to feed the negative momentum. You were creating positive loops, the results of which could only be positive, but you needed to keep stepping, and you did.

Three-quarters of the way through the case it became evident to me that there was a big positive kite coming through. But I just couldn't see what it was. It had yet to unfold. This kite couldn't come in until you pulled the case in. It would never have come in had you abandoned the case. It would have remained stuck behind something unfinished.

KELLIE:

You said that after seeing this through, something much bigger and better was coming in behind it, and you were right.

Despite the fact that the court case was raging, Kellie was creating positive momentum. This momentum was gaining ground. She had ignited a spark when she returned from Australia. Amid all the negativity she kindled the idea of working in the music industry. This little fire was starting to glow. I could see it flickering in the distance, but I could not get a good look at what it was. Kellie held firm. She held her fearful inner child close to her. She was brave and dealt with the resistance when it presented itself. It did present itself, in the form of the detectives. She had her wobble, but stayed on track. Her alignment with Source Energy was stronger than her fear. When she felt the fear, she acknowledged it, addressed it and stepped through it. She wasn't running away from it and because of all this there was something very exciting on the horizon.

VISUALISATION: CREATING MOMENTUM IN THE FIELD OF PURE POTENTIAL

Sit upright, and put a blanket over your shoulders if you like. Get comfortable, and listen to the ebb and flow of your beautiful breath, ebbing and flowing, ebbing and flowing. Let the tide of your breath lead you deep inside to where your inner child dwells. Softly approach her and hold her little hand. Tell her she is very safe and you are looking after her. Speak to her lovingly and tell her she is very important to you.

Now begin to explain to her that she is such an important part of the universe. You are telling your child things she has probably never heard before. Tell her that she is part of the delicate balance of the universe and this makes her very special. Ask her to close her eyes and visualise the universe as a large circle. You and your inner child are in the middle of this circle. The circle represents the universe and everything in it. This is the field of pure potential. Source Energy is the universe and that includes you and your inner child. The entire circle and everything in it is filled with pure potential and infinite intelligence. Tell her she is a very important part of this energy.

Explain to her that this energy weaves its way in and through her and everything in that circle. Ask her to release any worries and fears that are holding her back. As she releases this negativity it ripples out into the field of pure potential. As it ripples it disappears into nothingness.

It is time to increase momentum in your energetic and physical body. You will be able to do this through your chakras. Just bring your attention to the top of your head. This is your crown chakra. Imagine this chakra as the portal in fully accessing this stream of infinite intelligence. Visualise your crown chakra slightly opening in a clockwise motion. As it softens it is building momentum. This energetic swirling pool ripples out further and further. It is a sacred channel and this channel is now open. Pure energy starts to filter its way through you. It feels cool and light as it moves its way down, slowly soaking your body with energy. You may even see colours in your mind's eye as it begins to find its way through each chakra.

This crisp energy meanders gently to your third eye and then on to your throat. It is gradually creating momentum in both chakras. Your heart chakra reacts beautifully to this influx of magnificent energy and opens fully to it. As it moves on to your solar plexus and your sacral chakras, they begin to expand. Finally, the momentum in your root chakra starts to gather. This leaves you completely porous. Just like a sponge, you absorb this powerful energy. Your whole body feels light. The sense you have of your body ebbs away completely; you are totally immersed in the field of pure potential.

You feel as though you have dissolved into pure energy and you are now mingling in the field of pure potential. With each breath, every cell, organ and gland in your body is being revitalised. Your entire nervous system is being flushed and replenished with beautiful Source Energy. You are aligned and fully immersed in Source Energy. You know this is infinite intelligence and you have access to it.

You know what your wishes and desires are. You know what you want to bring into the physical world. Deeply embedded in you is the knowledge that all of what you want has already been conceived in the womb of your mind. This means that all your desires are here in this field of pure potential, and so are you. Pick one of your desires and allow yourself to feel it. If it is for more financial abundance, feel completely safe. Feel all your bills paid and all your worries looked after. Just allow yourself to feel a flow between you and your bills. Allow yourself to feel ease and flow. You don't have to wait until wealth comes into reality to start to feel it. Feel wealth right now in this energy space. Visualise yourself receiving wealth and it coming easily.

Now think of your other immediate desires. Know that your desires have been conceived already and they are here in the field of pure potential with you. Feel for the energy of it. If you cannot feel it yet, softly picture it in your mind. Momentum is picking up. Feel the joy starting to swell inside you at being able to sit in the presence of your desires in the inner reality of your imagination. As the momentum builds, you start to actually feel the energetic presence of your ideas and desires. They feel good and you now have access to them anytime you want.

Each time you access your desires in this energetic space, you are adding more and more momentum to them. Eventually the momentum increases to such a decree around your desires that they will be made manifest in your outer reality. Slowly, tell your inner child that it is time to come back. Start to feel your physical body and allow your chakras to close in gently. You now have the key to the door of the field of pure potential.

Each time you are in doubt and fear, just bring your inner child back to the field of pure potential that resides in your internal world. Tell her to ignore her outer situation for a few moments and allow her to play in this vast playground. All you have to do is close your eyes, relax and bring your attention to your crown chakra and open the door.

TOOLBOX

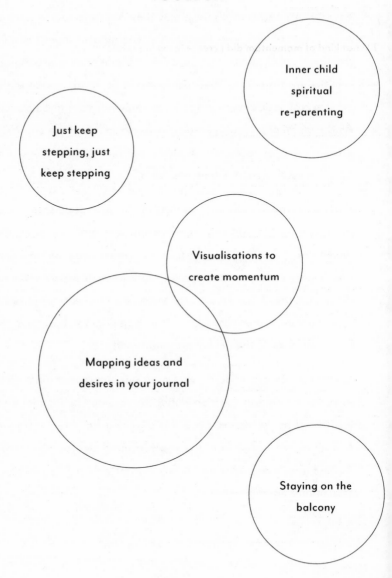

Inner child spiritual re-parenting

Just keep stepping, just keep stepping

Visualisations to create momentum

Mapping ideas and desires in your journal

Staying on the balcony

DIARY PAGES

1 What kind of momentum did I create in my life today?

2 List out the different types of momentum you created. For example, where did you create positive momentum? Where did you create negative momentum? Or did you create stop-start momentum?

3 Write down ways of creating momentum around your three desires. Know that the very act of writing this down is actually creating momentum in itself.

6

Receiving

'May I have the courage today to live
the life that I would love, to postpone my
dream no longer. But do at last what I
came here for and waste my heart on fear
no more.'

JOHN O'DONOHUE

Tuning in

THE ROOT CHAKRA

By now you probably don't need me to remind you to get cosy and relax your body. But this is your time now and you have co-created this beautiful sanctuary with Source Energy. So reach for your oils and light your candle. Place your hand on your heart and be with your lovely inner child. She needs you. Bring your attention gently to your root chakra. This is at the area at the base of your spine. This chakra is associated with grounding and prosperity. So get grounded and get ready to receive your abundance. Close your eyes and bring soft focus on this area of your body. While you are doing so, visualise the colour red. Now listen to the ebb and flow of your beautiful breath, ebbing and flowing, ebbing and flowing, ebbing and flowing ...

What you will learn from this chapter

—

In this chapter you will be taking a look at what it means to really receive in all its different guises. I will be explaining how you can form negative loops around giving and receiving things into your life. In truth you are receiving, spiritually, mentally, emotionally and physically, continuously. The chapter would not really be complete without a metaphor. So this time I will give a very short story about the magic porridge pot. We will go on to receive all of the metaphors illustrated in this book at a deep level by using your *f*ck it* decisions. In this chapter you will be saying farewell, for now, to Andrew and Kellie and I will share with you their stories of landing their individual kites. We will sit together and you will receive a deeply healing visualisation by bringing your inner child to the 'camp fire'. Your diary pages will be all about appreciation.

What does receiving mean?

—

Remember, you are the Holy Grail, you are a beautifully elaborate earthenware vessel ready to expand and receive limitless gifts from Source Energy. There are many different ways to receive. You are perpetually receiving – spiritually, mentally, emotionally and physically. Source Energy is continuous; it never switches off.

The act of receiving has a symbiotic relationship with the act of giving. This relationship is a continual ebb and flow, a constant give and take. One goes hand in hand with the other. This is how the universe is structured.

○ It is vital that you understand your thoughts and feelings about giving and receiving. In doing so you realise what kind of momentum you are creating. Is it positive momentum or negative momentum?

○ How you feel about receiving either increases abundance in your life or decreases it.

○ When you have figured out your relationship with giving and receiving, you can create in the awareness of what you are doing.

○ The important ingredient in successfully receiving is to appreciate all of what you *are* actually receiving.

Giving: more flow than ebb

—

Giving and receiving is a loaded subject. Some people are wonderful givers but cannot receive. They resist receiving because they do not think they are worthy to receive. These people, however, are big givers. They think it is everyone else's right to receive, but they themselves don't deserve it. They have programmed themselves with a negative pattern. Their inner child is being triggered each time they have to receive. Receiving becomes a closeted fear. Their inner child doesn't feel good enough, doesn't feel it is safe to receive and feels guilty in receiving. They end up giving, giving, giving in an endless loop, and wonder when it's their turn to receive. They also get resentful. In unawareness they repeat the same patterns over and over again, but they expect a different result; they expect to receive. They are in conflict with themselves. They are allowing their fearful inner child to direct the course of their lives and what they receive.

Others give to make themselves feel good. They receive gratitude from others and this feeds a big emptiness in them. They need to feel important

and at the centre of attention. This, again, goes back to their frightened little inner child. This inner child many not have received enough
attention in the formative years of life. Over time this child has learned
that giving is a big way to receive attention. They have created momentum
and an endless loop around this pattern. This is a negative loop of giving
and receiving and never fills the void they have inside them. This void
can only be filled by giving, where it is needed most. That means going
inwards and giving attention to the fearful inner child. In unawareness
this blocks them and they often attract people who will take advantage
of their giving. They, in turn, feed this because they need the attention.
Their fearful inner child has them caught in a perpetual cycle of negatively giving and negatively receiving. They give because of their need for
attention and they receive attention by being taken advantage of.

Giving: more ebb than flow
—

Then there are others whose inner child is afraid to give. They have
learned that it is not safe. Growing up, their inner child probably experienced lack on many levels. It could be the lack of love, understanding,
joy, health or money. They have experienced poverty on many levels.
I often feel this is a starvation, mentally, emotionally or physically, of
the different forms and expressions of love. They too carry this into
adulthood and severely restrict the ebb and flow of giving and receiving.
Everything seems measured, when in fact this is only their own inner
child keeping them stuck. They are blocking themselves from the flow of
abundance. This dynamic exchange needs to be fluid and unrestricted;
this keeps abundance circulating in our lives. If someone is afraid to give
they run the risk of restricting their flow of abundance greatly.

There are also individuals who only want to receive and not give at all. This is another pattern established out of fear. It is a major stumbling block to allowing abundance to flow and quite often keeps people very stuck.

NO MATTER WHAT PATTERN YOU HAVE ENTRENCHED IN YOUR MIND, IF IT IS A NEGATIVE PATTERN ASSOCIATED WITH RECEIVING, YOU MUST ADDRESS IT WITH YOUR INNER CHILD, because this is all it is, a learned behavioural pattern. It is your perceived reality based on outdated files that you have stored in the computer bank of your mind. But you can change things by recognising it, acknowledging it and working with the fearful inner child in reprogramming your mind.

The entire process of receiving

—

It is the entire process of co-creating with Source Energy that is so enjoyable. This joy is present on every step of the journey, from starting out with minuscule knowing or feeling to arriving at your destination of full realisation. By the time you receive physically, the journey is nearly done – this process started when you were receiving spiritually, emotionally and mentally. While no one can deny that the actual receiving of an idea is magnificent, the truth is that the whole journey is magnificent, from conception to birth.

For a moment imagine you are Michelangelo's prize student. He is working on a sculptural masterpiece and invites you to co-create it with him. While you are more than excited to see the masterpiece finished, you are also enjoying working with such a great and skilful creator, and learning a lot on the way. It is not just seeing the masterpiece finished that's important; it is the journey to the finish.

RECEIVING SPIRITUALLY

This is the most important level. Without receiving from this level you would not exist. You are an energetic being first and foremost. In fact the earth and all its inhabitants and the universe itself would not exist if it didn't constantly receive from Source Energy. Source Energy infuses everything. I love the Hebrew word *ruah*, the breath of life. This breath is not just for us human beings but for the entire universe. In the bigger picture everything is done for us. The moon and stars stay in the sky; the tides ebb and flow; the seasons turn.

You have the ability to increase what you receive. This is done by using all the gifts Source Energy has already given you. Remember the relationship between giving and receiving. Deciding to step into 'who you really are' means that you are using what you have. You have to use what you have been given first. Stepping into your full potential and owning who you are opens the way for more to be given to you.

RECEIVING MENTALLY AND EMOTIONALLY

As you align with Source Energy, you begin to receive mentally. You are open and asking for clarity, asking for intuitive guidance and asking for ideas and inspiration.

You begin to move in more awareness, starting to consciously direct your subconscious mind. Bit by bit you become more mindful of how important it is to stand on the balcony of your life and observe yourself mentally. What are you thinking? If you are thinking negatively in unawareness you will create negatively and then wonder why this is always happening to you. If you create deliberately in awareness you begin to co-create with Source Energy the life you want to live. Don't worry if you catch yourself going into negative chit-chat in your head. In fact, you should celebrate because this means that you have noticed it and are now more consciously aware and can direct your thoughts more clearly and positively. (The tool of your inner child is very important here.)

The benefits of receiving mentally include:

O an improved connection with Source Energy, which enables you to receive full access to the field of pure potential (you can create what you want),

O more capacity to receive and conceive your ideas and desires,

O heightened intuition, greater clarity.

Mentally receiving is interconnected with emotionally receiving. You are receiving energetically from others all the time. You are picking up vibes from the people you love very much and people you don't love as much. You are picking up on their emotions and feelings. You can decide what you want to receive.

Remember:

O I will practise standing on the balcony of my life.

O I will observe my emotions, my thoughts, feelings, words, body language and actions.

O I will look after my inner child. Hand on heart.

O I will choose the emotions and feelings I want to conjure up.

RECEIVING PHYSICALLY

How you receive physically would fill an infinite number of books. It is deeply affected by how you receive mentally and emotionally. Here are just a few examples of how you receive countless gifts every day. *Ruah*, the breath of life, is the most precious of gifts and is often completely taken for granted. Have you ever had the privilege of sitting with someone as they prepared to pass from this life? Each breath is consciously appreciated and eagerly waited for. You feel huge relief when the next breath comes until finally there are no more.

Other gifts from Source Energy include air, water, food, sky, land, sea, children, family, lovers, friends, animals – the list is endless. The health, wealth, joy and happiness infused within your being is a huge gift from Source Energy. Every time we receive pleasure, whether from a smile, laughter or a kind gesture, Source Energy is giving to us.

'Freely you have received; freely give.' – MATTHEW 10:8 In your diary page at the end of this chapter, make your own list of what you receive on the bigger (macro) scale and also on the smaller (micro) scale. These lists of gratitude and appreciation are tools in your toolbox to keep you aligned and tuned in to Source Energy. By making these lists you increase momentum, amplify appreciation and release resistance, making it much easier for your kites to come in to land.

The magic porridge pot

—

Do you remember the children's story of the magic porridge pot? This is the perfect story to illustrate the overflowing abundance of Source Energy that lives within. Let me remind you briefly.

There was once a little girl and her mother living on the edge of a forest. They were poor and had no food to eat. In desperation the little girl went into the forest to look for food. While she was there she met an old woman who was aware of her poverty and gave her a little pot. She told her it would cook lovely sweet porridge and all she had to do was say 'Cook, little pot, cook', and when she wanted it to stop all she had to say was 'Stop, little pot, stop.' The little girl took it home to her mother and they had plenty to eat. One day her mother was using the pot and forgot to say, 'Stop, little pot, stop.' The porridge flowed and flowed, rippling out to the entire village and beyond ...

Now imagine that this magic pot of energy is inside you and has always been inside you, but you didn't realise it. You have already received it and it has been yours for eternity. This is the well of Source Energy within you. It has been waiting patiently for you to use it. When it is finally acknowledged and you are consciously aware that it exists in you, it begins to bubble up. Meditation will help you receive the awareness of this wonderful little pot inside you. All this little pot of energy needs is your magic words. These magic words come from your conscious mind, mindfully directing your subconscious mind, telling it what to do.

Once you give the right instructions to your magic pot of energy, it starts to flow and flow. You can stop it if you like, speed it up or slow it down. But if you just let your pot of energy flow inside you, there is no limit to how far it can ripple out.

Receiving the metaphors

—

Your subconscious mind is now really resonating with the metaphors that I have used in each chapter. You are subliminally receiving these stories and pictures, and you are conjuring them up in your mind. Your subconscious will accept this information more quickly and start to act immediately on what has been given to it. You are receiving constantly, even while you are reading, and you are barely realising it.

Come and stand on the balcony with me and we will view all the ways you are receiving and can receive. Standing on the balcony enables you to be consciously aware of what's going on in your life, and gives you a sneak preview of the bigger picture. You are now appreciating and receiving all the tools I am offering to you. Sewn intricately within the fabric of these beautiful processes is the knowledge of creating your own reality in awareness with Source Energy.

Together, we are going to make seven *f*ck it* decisions in this chapter, and put them in our toolbox. Know and trust that you will carry this information in your subconscious mind from now on. There is no room for doubt; it slows you down.

REVISITING THE KITE METAPHOR

Say this first decision out loud with feeling:

1 '*F*ck it* ... I am allowing myself to receive.'

You are standing with many strings in your hands of all the kites you wish to pull in. There will be many kites throughout your lifetime. You are holding the strings of your personal purpose kite and your higher purpose kite too. Some of these kites are big and extraordinary; others are smaller and more ordinary. All of these kites represent your desires, wishes and dreams. As soon as you land a kite, another one forms way off in the distance. Even before you can see it you have the string in your hand. Your connection to your kites is absolute. No one can take these kites away from you. Sooner or later, all your kites will come in to land, as long as you don't block them with resistance. You now know this.

You are now aware that resistance is fear. This fear is stored deep in the recesses of your mind and is represented by your fearful inner child. This fearful little one does not have a good opinion of herself. She has been conditioned to think the worst. Your distant kites are in danger of staying out in the stratosphere, and never gaining momentum or coming home to land, when you expose them to negative forces. This negativity can come from your own inner child or that of another. You are more consciously aware and have been honing your craft with regard to deliberately creating your own reality. You now know what causes resistance.

Always align yourself with Source Energy first; this ensures that you will receive your kites and bring them home to land. Know that you have your desires in the palm of your hand, and feel the strings gently pulling your kites in little by little. When the desire gets stuck through fear, acknowledge this and ease your way through it step by step, creating positive momentum as you go. There is no joy in strangling yourself with the string of a kite that is stuck in a tree, or struggling to pull it in. Decide and expect to untangle and unravel any negativity and old conditioning. Always remember to pull in the nearest kites first, otherwise the kites further away will not be able to land. Then, with skill rather than effort, with joy rather than fear, in awareness rather than unawareness, pull your creation successfully in to land and receive it with appreciation. You now know what to do with resistance.

REVISITING THE RADIO STATION

Alignment to Source Energy is the key to success. You need to tune yourself in to the frequency of Source Energy. Through the processes you have been exposed to while reading this book you have been gradually tuning yourself in bit by bit. Fiddling with your radio dial bit by bit moves you closer to your desired station. All the while you have been feeling, visualising, imagining and meditating your way into alignment. You are creating momentum and emphatically deciding, '*F*ck it*, I don't want to be tuned out any more.' You are consciously aware that there is a better station you could be enjoying, you know it exists and you fully expect to find it. You are aware that there may be interference on the way and you allow for this. You may not be tuned in all the time, but you are not giving up. You are nearer to it than you have ever been, and when you tune yourself in you know you will receive clear reception. Once you have experienced the frequency of this station you will never want to tune out of it again. Say the second decision out loud.

    2 '*F*ck it* ... Source Energy is the station I *am* tuning into.'

REVISITING THE EMBRYO CONCEPT

Metaphorically speaking, Source Energy holds the universe in the womb of its mind. Source Energy is magnificently creative and abundant, lush and fertile. You are in symbiotic union with this pulsating energy. This energy is within you. It has to be, otherwise you would simply not exist. You receive its grace every second of your life and you have the ability to continuously co-create with it. You have limitless potential and you are abundant beyond belief. This powerful energy expresses itself through you at all times.

O Aligning with Source Energy opens you up to the limitless possibilities that lie in the field of pure potential.

O The split second an idea has entered your mind it has been conceived.

O This is where the divine and human meet.

O Doubts and fears cause resistance and restrict momentum from gaining around your embryotic ideas.

- It is vital to ignore your outer circumstances; pay more attention to the idea forming deep within you.

- Just like cell division, your embryonic idea amasses and multiplies in the womb of your mind.

- When the momentum increases to such a degree, it takes on a life of its own.

- Remember, your ideas have a gestation period.

- If a desire is born prematurely it may not survive.

- Ideas need to be nurtured, not forced.

- When they are fully ready they will finally be born into a new reality.

- In giving birth to anything, you need to prepare yourself to let go of all resistance and fear.

- You also need to prepare yourself to receive the fruits of your labours.

> **3** '*F*ck it* ... Source Energy is always within me no matter what I have done.'

REVISITING THE CREATIVE PROCESS

- During the first trimester, your idea/desire is conceived by aligning with Source Energy. Meditation is the big tool to use at this part of the process.

- During the second trimester, your idea/desire is nurtured within the womb of your mind. Your inner child practice is a big tool to use at this part of the process.

- During the third trimester, your idea/desire is gaining momentum and preparing for birth by releasing resistance. Your big tools here are your inner child practice and meditation.

4 '*F*ck it* ... from this moment on I am creating my own reality in awareness.'

Remember what I said earlier: it is far easier to create a million euro than to create a brain or a heart, yet this is how women and men co-create with Source Energy every day of the week. You are co-creating with Source Energy every second of the day, but you are mostly unaware of this. Now you are stepping into conscious awareness of the fact that you are a co-creator in alignment with Source Energy and you have full access to the field of pure potential. Make sure you are ready to receive its many blessings.

5 '*F*ck it* ... I *am* ready to receive all the blessings Source Energy gives me.'

REVISITING THE SUPERCOMPUTER

We are constantly connected to and receiving information from the supercomputer that is Source Energy. Not only does this vast mind of Source Energy store universal data, it allows you to access it at will. The speed at which you receive this data is in accordance with how established your connection is to it. Sometimes resistance can block your way. When you choose to minimise or close old tabs, the connection improves and you gain faster access to new information. You are upgrading your operating system. By aligning with Source Energy you gain access to infinite intelligence; when you emit a clear signal, Source Energy always responds. You are always capable of receiving, because once you ask, you will receive – providing you don't block it. Say the sixth decision out loud.

6 '*F*ck it* ... I am minimising and closing all outdated files.'

Sometimes your mind can get too congested. This slows down the whole process of deliberately co-creating with Source Energy. This is when it is vital to have a meditation practice. It is a myth that you don't have time to meditate – you are actually wasting time by not meditating. You need to make sure that your connection to the supercomputer is clear. When the signal is clear you will receive updates of what's going on within you all the time. Your internal computer will give you an accurate reading in the form of your intuition, emotions, feelings and knowing.

7 '*F*ck it* ... I *am* listening to the information I receive from Source Energy at all times.'

Brilliant! Those seven decisions are powerful and you have fully received them. Well done! Now let's look how Andrew and Kelly and I opened ourselves to receiving.

JUDITH

In my story you can see my deep desires and how they formed as a child. You can trace how I moved away from alignment with Source Energy and stopped listening to my own intuition, building negative momentum. Then I started to listen and tuned myself back to into alignment, making *f*ck it* decisions to create my own positive reality in awareness. Finally, you can see some of the results I have had to date, all by using the processes I have outlined in this book.

When I was a child, like all small children I was receiving constantly from Source Energy and I didn't think twice about it. My connection with this energy was very strong. I always knew I could go straight to this infinite intelligence whenever I needed to.

As children we absorb what is around us; for me, during the 70s and 80s I became aware of differences in gender. Growing up I felt I was automatically restricted because I was female. In my childhood patriarchal dominance was rife. Society was governed by men. So, not surprisingly and not unlike Andrew, equality was becoming an issue for me.

During my youth the conflicts that never ceased to trouble me were the controversies surrounding the Catholic Church and how the patriarchy treated women. As I said earlier, I was coming to the conclusion that there was nothing in the Church for me as a woman. However, throughout this period Source Energy was ever-present inside me. I couldn't understand it. My internal God was all-embracing; the external God was a God of dominance.

Then there was that period in my life when I lost my confidence. I began to slowly inch away from alignment. I was tuning out from Source Energy in unawareness; my fearful inner child was beginning to take charge of my life. But Source Energy never stopped whispering.

Finally, I couldn't contain what was inside me any longer. I was starting to receive the signal much more clearly now, and I was finally starting to listen to my intuition and tune in again. However, my inner fearful child was going ballistic. I made a very important decision. *F*ck it*; I decided I was going to take the steering wheel of my life gently from this fearful child and I was going to be the one to drive. I decided to come back to Dublin with my three wonderful children and began to create my own reality in more awareness on my own. I had stopped resisting who I was. This had been a major block and now my kites were starting to land one after another.

I made big *f*ck it* decisions:

O *F*ck it* – I was going to create my own abundant reality.

O *F*ck it* – I was going to use my gifts of intuition, creativity and intelligence.

O *F*ck it* – I wasn't going to let being a woman in this world stop me any longer.

O *F*ck it* – I wasn't yielding to society and all its outdated expectations.

I was a woman of the twenty-first century. I didn't have to be someone who stood between two worlds. I didn't have to have one foot in the ideology of a pre-Vatican II era and the other foot in a post-Vatican II era. I could stand with both feet firmly planted in truth. But my internal truth and the external truth still didn't marry up. What was the truth? I wanted to receive the truth. It was an integral part of my jigsaw puzzle.

Shockingly for me, it was within this structure of the patriarchy that I found my liberation. When I began my studies in theology it was here, amid centuries of male dominance, I received my truth. Not only that, but the truth was eagerly given to me. I didn't have to fight for it. I was helped, supported and nurtured every step of the way. As I said earlier, it was here I found Sophia. Everything made complete sense to me: the internal battle between female and male, dominance and control; my internal relationship with Source Energy and the external tyrannical androcentric God – it all came together. The biblical Sophia, wisdom, the feminine expression of the presence of God – I had found the balance, yin and yang. Hallelujah! I felt as though a big secret had been unveiled and I felt verified. Women and men had suffered because of an out-of-balance mindset. It has left its mark on both sexes. But I now realised it didn't have to be an indelible mark. Yet another big block was removed, leaving my kites to freely come in now that I was really beginning to flow.

Over the last seven years I have developed the seven processes you have read about in this book. I am constantly amazed at how things happen so fast when you co-create with Source Energy. Things have really accelerated for me. I have fine-tuned these processes and I am delighted to share them with you. I have used them to create my own reality. The more I practise them, the more momentum gathers and the more I receive.

I began receiving and accepting myself, acknowledging my inner child and loving her unconditionally. I released my internal resistances, blocks and fears from my conditioning that were holding me back. I am completely allowing Source Energy to work within me. I have experienced the powerful positive results of this and I love it. My children are thriving and I am in abundance with wonderful people in my life. I have also completed my honours degree in theology.

As for my business, well, it is flourishing. I have gratefully received this book from Source Energy and it is only the beginning of a new chapter in my life. I started with one client seven years ago and my journey has led me to running workshops and seminars on how to deliberately create your own reality, in conjunction with fertility workshops for women and men.

I am now being led into my higher purpose. For me this involves a heart-felt desire for humanity to realise a transcendent level of knowledge beyond the traditional images of God, female or male. I am committed to co-creating with this energy and to living fully from the field of pure potential as opposed to accessing it occasionally. This is a work in progress and I am hugely enjoying my journey co-creating with Source Energy.

Once you acknowledge who you are, align yourself with Source Energy and clear any resistance, you are worthy to receive.

Join myself and Andrew in standing on the balcony and observing how he led himself from creating in unawareness to becoming a deliberate co-creator with Source Energy and the outcome he received.

ANDREW

I can see what I have created clearly now. I think civil rights were, metaphorically speaking, encoded in my genes, in my lineage through my great-grandparents. From the age of four to seventeen I was seriously bullied, so the feelings of equality grew and grew within. Unbeknownst to me, I built more momentum around this when I went to college to study equality in UCD. My twenties were the best and worst times of my life. During my twenties I suffered panic attacks and that was because I was trying to please other people, and not looking after myself.

Then the momentum really started to gather when I was thirty and I began to step in more awareness. I remember having a massive panic attack, and I thought,'I cannot do this anymore, this is not for me'. A friend of mine had died, among other things, and it set off this massive panic. That probably was the point when I started stepping into something that was for me.

JUDITH:

In effect, Andrew, you made an enormous f*ck it decision, probably the most important decision of your life; you came out as being a gay man. You began to step into your own power. Not an easy thing to do. When you go against what is socially acceptable, you can expect the wrath of a man-made god to descend on you.

You began to use the processes I have outlined here and mindfully kept yourself aligned with Source Energy. You were turning towards that inner light and you were not trying to hide it. You began to allow Source Energy to express itself through you more fully. This powerful energy can only do that if you allow it. That meant having the courage to let go of your resistance. That frightened little boy inside you was so wounded but you took time to acknowledge him. You had decided to let it all go and step into your full power. You had to do this otherwise you could not have stepped into your higher purpose. At the time that higher purpose was the marriage equality referendum.

ANDREW:

Yes, the campaign was all about love. We used to say that our love was the same as any other love. Essentially it was a real campaign about love. Because you have to remember as a gay person you are being told that you cannot have love. You will never have love, and or if you do, it will never be recognised.

JUDITH:

So you built huge internal momentum around equality and love all your life. The idea was conceived in the womb of your mind since childhood, and you released enough resistance so that it could be borne out into reality in many ways, eventually taking shape with the marriage equality campaign and referendum.

ANDREW:

Absolutely. And then just before the vote was cast, in one of my sessions with you, we focused on the mantra, 'you can do anything now'. This was really important to me. I think at that stage I knew, in terms of the referendum, and in my life in general, if you set your heart to it, and if it is really what you want, you can do anything. The other mantra was 'release the outcome'. This was really important because I realised, regardless of the outcome of the vote, we had changed Ireland because of the conversations that had taken place. So 'release the outcome' was

*akin to 'f*ck it, we will do this – win or lose, we're doing it anyway'. We knew why
we were doing it, and we knew what we were doing was right.*

*People often ask me, what was my biggest learning throughout the campaign?
They expect a corporate reply about how I liaised with politicians or something
like that. I reply 'ego', and I always get a puzzled look. I learned about my ego and
everybody else's and that was through releasing the outcome.*

JUDITH:

*Standing on the balcony gave you a god's-eye view. This was of your fearful
inner child and the frightened little child within those around you. It allowed
you compassion and understanding for both yourself and others. It minimised
resistance and kept everything flowing. Instead of reacting with fear to other
people's homophobia, you reacted in awareness of the fears that were being
brought up for everyone.*

ANDREW:

*Yes, it allowed me to move forward in a more productive way, from a higher
perspective. I began to celebrate the small wins. The changes that were occurring
in people emotionally moved me, the broadening of people's minds and the
beginnings of solidarity. So, honestly, by the time we came to the end, I had
celebrated all the wins. These were the wins in people's hearts. It was a rich
experience. Don't get me wrong, I bawled my eyes out when the yes vote came in
on 22 May 2015.*

JUDITH:

*Andrew, after you and your colleagues landed the marriage equality kite, other
kites were waiting patiently behind it. Can I share with the reader?*

ANDREW:

Yes, sure, go ahead.

The two things Andrew desired most of all in his life were equality and love. These kites most certainly landed for him. He had to manifest and feel them internally first to enable him to fulfil his personal purpose. Then he co-created them externally on a grand scale. This led him to fulfil his higher purpose in this regard. There are many other things Andrew will co-create in his long life, as he has a lot of strings of many kites in his hands yet to come. This I know, but I will leave it as a surprise for him.

I am going to tell some tales now! Andrew is a wonderful creator. After the referendum a lot of Andrew's fabulous kites came in to land. This included a very welcomed, but unexpected one: a wonderful partner. They are just two ordinary people like you and me, but they are allowing Source Energy to flow through them, and because of that they are co-creating extraordinary lives.

KELLIE

Kellie's accident catapulted her out of alignment and straight into fear. You can feel the fear when you read her words: 'All I could hear were the brakes of a car screeching on the wet surface, and I'm thinking I've just been hit by a car, or a bus, please don't be a bus. I'm on Bondi Road in Sydney and I cannot die here.'

In her shocked state, suffering from post-traumatic stress, she had to make some serious f*ck it decisions – to leave Australia, her relationship, her job, her life and come home to Ireland. She decided not to run to London to escape herself, to stay home and go internally to her distraught inner child and heal. She decided bravely to continue with a harrowing court case, and while in the midst of this, planted the seeds of hope. In the middle of such chaos she was paving the way for her future. That takes great courage and trust.

Due to her efforts at keeping herself aligned in her darkest of hours, she was gaining more and more access to the field of pure potential. This was allowing Kellie to receive the ideas that had been conceived when she returned to Dublin. Her idea of working in the music industry had been nurtured. It was being nurtured in the womb of her mind. All the meditation, walking and mindfulness had fed this embryonic idea. Through our work together Kellie knew that tuning in to Source Energy makes you receptive and gives you great clarity.

She was stepping herself through the court case. She was being bullied in many ways but she was releasing the outcome, staying aligned with Source Energy and building momentum around as much positivity as she could during the court case.

KELLIE:

With regard to the court case, I could have seen it all through and nothing would have come of it. I was seeing it through completely with no guarantee of a positive outcome for me.

JUDITH:

You were just doing what you were intuitively being guided to do, and you went with your intuition all the time. That was Source Energy working through you. You were receptive and listened. It was always guaranteed to have the best possible outcome for you, for your highest good, one way or the other. You have to understand that what is created with positivity can only have a positive outcome. Even though the court case in itself was negative you had decided to conduct yourself positively and chose to stay aligned.

Therefore in the end what you received from it, on many levels, had to be positive. Not just the outcome of the case in itself, but all the wonderful inner gifts and strengths you received while stepping yourself through it. That is why

I said 'release the outcome'. There was the smaller picture of the outcome and the bigger picture of how you were going to let it shape the rest of your life. I told Andrew to release the outcome too and I also do that for myself in my journeys. The mantra was 'release the outcome' and concentrate on the journey. Concentrate on stepping through it aligned with Source Energy and the outcome will be good.

Kellie did 'release the outcome' of the court case and just kept to the plan. She had to return to Australia to attend court, and in doing so she faced many fears. But all the time she held tightly to her alignment. Holding on to hope, positivity and her intuition every day, she never gave up. Eventually she had built up so much positive momentum it burst out into the physical. She won her court case, but most important, she stepped through her fear. This led on to an even bigger kite landing and that was the mysterious kite, way up in the stratosphere, we had had a sense of many months before.

She had conceived this desire in her darkest of hours. She had nurtured it carefully, not speaking about it in depth to anyone but me. She put light focus on it and meditated softly around it. She had cleared all the tangled negative kites and made way for it to land. Out of the apparent chaos she had kept this kite free of negativity. Forming momentum slowly around it, her creation was sensitively dependent on the conditions and the conditions were good. Some kind of order was forming in the midst of apparent disorder. Source Energy was at work. All her diligent aligning was about to pay off and the momentum in her life was set to increase in no small way.

KELLIE:

I had done the energetic work and anything I was guided to do in the physical. I kept myself aligned and released my resistance and fear. Then I just surrendered, and opened to receiving whatever came. It was then it all fell into place. An incredible opportunity popped up and that was to tour the world with one of the biggest bands in the world. The job presented itself through a contact I didn't even know I had. I went through the interviewing process with them and started shortly after the court case was finished. It was an incredible opportunity.

JUDITH:

Yes, I remember. That mysterious kite that I had seen way off was coming closer and closer during the court case. You had the two kites landing, so to speak, more or less at the same time. The court case kite and the job kite. It was great to watch you skilfully pull the strings of both. You just kept on working on your alignment and trusted completely that mighty connection you have to Source Energy through your intuition. The positive momentum was building. You released the outcome and just enjoyed the feeling through the process.

Kellie was resilient. The most important thing she did throughout her process was to work on her alignment. She released herself from the grip of shock and post-traumatic stress. Then she landed a successful outcome in her court case, but more important, she released the fears around stepping through it. Finally she landed an absolutely fantastic job and travelled the world. She did this in a very short space of time, and she was focused. Kellie is continuously creating her own reality with Source Energy, and she is getting better and better at it. Kellie, like Andrew and me, is just an ordinary person deliberately creating an extraordinary life.

Revisiting the seven decisions

—

There is a technique that suggests if you hold a thought and a feeling for a few seconds, you will start to align with that reality. So, using our toolbox, let's revisit the seven *f*ck it* decisions we have made in this chapter. We will hold each decision for 17 seconds. This allows you to build up feeling and momentum around each decision. You might even be amused at how emphatic you are when you are saying your *f*ck it* decisions out loud and with feeling. You are now successfully programming your subconscious mind and it's easy. In fact, it is fun! Let your inner child play – you are allowed.

From this moment on, no more shame, no more guilt, no more anger, no more pain, no more lack, no more fear and no more criticism. You have done enough of all of that. Generations of conditioning has caused negative thoughts in our collective unconscious. The words 'I am not worthy to receive you' have deep-rooted and important religious meaning. However, without clear explanation and interpretation, they also programme the collective mind unconsciously and negatively, much as TV commercials do. So beware of those TV commercials that underline sickness, negativity or violence, and instead look towards appreciation and gratitude. Appreciation and gratitude are powerful tools. Make your mental and physical lists of appreciation often. This raises your energy and helps keep you aligned.

VISUALISATION: THE INNER CHILD

In this visualisation we will be bringing your inner child on a little journey to a lovely camp fire. This will help you to release anything that has been worrying or troubling you over the years. Any negativity you are holding on to is blocking your way. So allow your inner child to be free and tell her to throw it all in the camp fire. In releasing the resistance, we are preparing the way for you to receive.

Retreat to your comfort zone. You will always be able to come here whenever you like, even long after you finish reading this book. Make sure you are comfortable and warm, look lovingly at your photo of you as a child. You are safe. Listen to your breath ebbing and flowing, ebbing and flowing, ebbing and flowing. Let your breath bring you deep inside yourself where your inner child resides.

She is a beautiful child, full of wonderful potential. She is very loving and kind. But this child is wounded and fearful. There are many things that have upset her and have never been acknowledged. They have held her in fear and she is afraid to move forwards. She has worries and fears that she has wanted to talk to you about over the years. But you have ignored her. She has been crying on her own, scared, with no one to listen to her.

Sit beside her for a few minutes. Hold her little hand and slowly bend down to look into her beautiful eyes. Tell her that you are so very sorry. You didn't realise you were ignoring her. You were in unawareness, and just didn't realise what you were doing. Promise her that from now on she is the most important person in your life. Tell her you will listen to her. Look after her and love her from now on.

Explain gently that it is time she let go of all her fears. Tell her you are going to help her with that. Encourage her to trust you and while holding her little hand, begin to walk with her. As you walk, you come across a camp fire. It is very warm and inviting, so you decide to sit with her beside the fire. While you sit warming yourself, you notice a small dusty box beside the child. It is an old worn-out box of memories and it belongs to the child. It contains all her worries and fears. All the times she felt alone and the times she was scared. Even all the times she caused pain to others. This box is full of old negative emotions and feelings and the child still carries them around with her. There is no more room in the box for her to receive new things.

Now ask the child if she would be willing to let some of what is in the box go. Ask her if she could throw just a few of the smaller things that she doesn't need into the fire. Tell her it could be like a little game. She might even enjoy seeing how the old stuff goes up in a puff of smoke, or creates a fabulous glow as it burns. Coax her to let go.

See your child slowly throw some smaller things from her childhood into the fire. Encourage her, and ask her to throw anything from when she was a teenager into the fire too. She is starting to enjoy the process and is keen to get rid of some more old stuff. Ask her if there is anything painful around relationships in the box that she would consider letting go. Anything negative around her mother or father, or any of her family – tell her, it's okay, just pop it in the fire. Allow her to put as much as she likes into the fire. If she slows up, ask her to look deeper into the box and see if there is anything else to go. Encourage her to release times when she was hurt or when she hurt others. Cajole her to let go of anger or resentment. Tell her to take this opportunity to get rid of as much as she can. See the fire glow as she keeps throwing things on it.

Cuddle her, telling her she is just brilliant and you love her very much. Tell her you are very proud of her. It is not easy to let go of things you have had for a long time, even if they are negative. She has really done well. Reach out for her hand again and slowly stand up. As you start to walk, you see the most beautiful light ahead. Picking up the little child you start to walk purposefully towards the light. In fact it is so inviting the two of you go straight into it. As you do, you are immersed in clear, crisp energy. You feel a deep sense of love and joy. You are engulfed in pure consciousness and every cell in your body is filled with the light of infinite intelligence.

Breathe this into you. Feel this crisp, clear energy enter every cell in your body. Breathe this unconditional love into all organs and glands in your body. See this powerfully strong and abundant energy ripple out from you into your auric fields. Feel it like silver ripples flowing out toward the people you love. See this powerful, strong, abundant, limitless energy ripple further out to all the people you work with and all your friends. This strong flow of energy reaches out to all the people you haven't met yet. All the projects and ideas and desires that are in your field of pure potential are now fused with this energy. On and on this energy ripples out, to Mother Earth and the universe.

Now breathe this energy back into you. Breathe this universal energy in. You are one with the universe, you are powerful, you are strong, and you are unconditional love. You are limitless and you are abundant. This is who you really are. You have fully received Source Energy into your life and you are aligned.

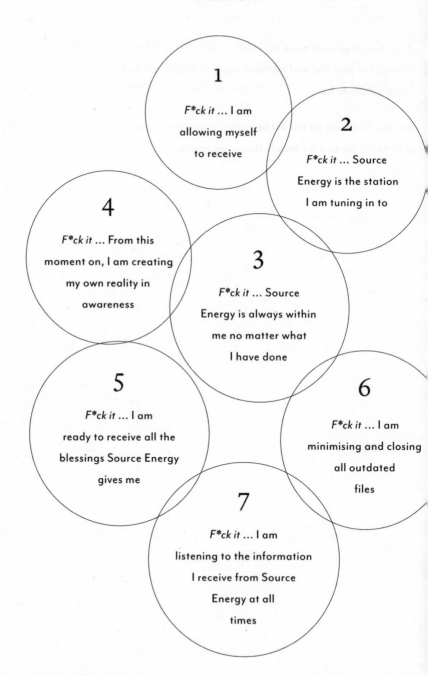

1

F*ck it … I am allowing myself to receive

2

F*ck it … Source Energy is the station I am tuning in to

4

F*ck it … From this moment on, I am creating my own reality in awareness

3

F*ck it … Source Energy is always within me no matter what I have done

5

F*ck it … I am ready to receive all the blessings Source Energy gives me

6

F*ck it … I am minimising and closing all outdated files

7

F*ck it … I am listening to the information I receive from Source Energy at all times

DIARY PAGES

1 On this page write out a list of all the wonderful things you have received in your life, and all the things you appreciate and have deep gratitude for.

Let the first thing on this list be appreciation for your own wonderful life and the breath that you breathe.

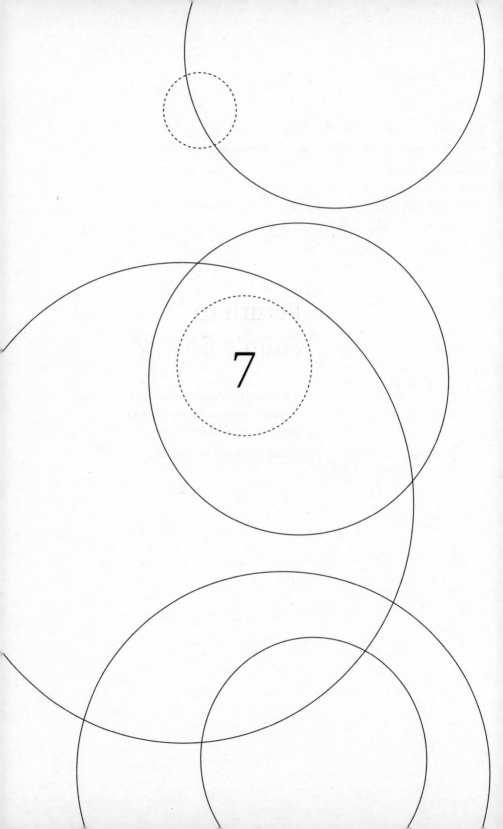

7

Return to Source Energy

'We are not human beings having a
spiritual experience. We are spiritual
beings having a human experience.'

PIERRE TEILHARD DE CHARDIN

Tuning in

THE CROWN CHAKRA

Close your eyes, feel your body, and release all tension within you. Listen to the ebb and flow of your breath, ebbing and flowing, ebbing and flowing, ebbing and flowing. Bring your attention to your crown chakra at the top of your head. Feel this chakra gently open and begin to spiral in a clockwise motion. Feel your connection with Source Energy forming, that silver cord of crisp vibrant energy connecting you to the field of pure potential. Know that there are others in this space with you. You are not alone and you feel very safe. Gently put your hand on your heart and direct your wonderful inner child. Tell her clearly and lovingly what you want, what is your heart's desire. Out loud, tell her what you want her to do, and tell her, 'this is now done'. Tell her you love her. Be emphatic and trust that your instructions will be acted on.

Now feel the energy from the silver cord run down to your third eye. As this energy illuminates your third eye, tell your child, 'I have decided I am using my intuition at all times,' giving her gentle but firm direction. Then feel this clear energy in your throat. This is unblocking any resistance. Again direct your inner child, saying, 'I have decided I am expressing myself through joy.' As it passes into your heart chakra, your chest expands and you feel loved. Directing your little child, you tell her, 'I have decided that you come first and I love you unconditionally.' When it reaches your solar plexus you are empowered. Say softly to your child, 'I have decided to stand in my personal power, I am strong.' As the energy floods your sacral chakra, you tell your inner child, 'I have decided I am a wonderful co-creator with Source Energy.' Finally, as it reaches your root chakra, tell your little child, 'I have decided to play and have fun, I am very safe and secure in this world.'

See and feel the silver cord moving out from your root chakra. As it does, it penetrates the earth deeply. This grounds you to Mother Earth. You are now perfectly balanced between the heavens and the earth. You have set your intention personally, but this intention has also been set amid the collective consciousness that has now gathered. You have given clear instruction to your subconscious mind through the powerful tool of your inner child. Your desires are gently gaining momentum in the womb of your mind.

What you will learn from this chapter

—

In Part One, I said there were two important characters in this book: one was Source Energy and the other was You. The two are inextricably intertwined. Your journey began with the chapter 'Connect to Source Energy' and it is completed in this chapter. You have come full circle. We are all part of a collective consciousness so, bearing that in mind, in a few moments we will do a tuning in. This time the tuning in isn't as personal as the ones in previous chapters. In a sense we will be going beyond ourselves, accessing the collective consciousness. Tapping into this amplifies the energy, opening the way even further and gathering more momentum for your continued health, wealth, joy and happiness. Then I will lead you through the consolidation of all seven practices and move into the bigger picture and a collective higher purpose. Finally I will share with you some daily practice and tools you can use moving forwards to stay aligned with Source Energy.

The significance of tuning in

—

When I was writing the tuning in paragraph in each chapter, I would visualise us all as a group together. I would sit and feel this wonderful Source Energy emanating out from all of us collectively. Remember, when you feel something deeply, your subconscious mind cannot tell whether or not it's physically happening. If you feel it, and direct your subconscious to it, it will have to play out.

I purposely chose to open a chakra in each tuning in. Using all the tools I could while writing each chapter makes the information very accessible to you on all levels of your being. Meditation, visualisation, imagination, breathing and relaxing were but a few of these tools. I repeated certain things deliberately. This gathers positive momentum around a positive habit. Tuning in has now become part of reading this book for you. Don't let it stop here. Now that you have established the habit, use it every time you read any book. Or any time you get a moment during the day to sit quietly. Even if it is only outside your office, in the car, before you go into work.

For those of you who say you don't or can't meditate, if you have been doing the tuning in, you have been tentatively meditating. If you really have made a decision to deliberately co-create your own reality, keep feeding this habit. You can tap into that feeling over and over again, whenever you like. All you have to do is sit comfortably. Then relax your body, your jaw and your brow. Then release the tension from your shoulders. You will hear me say, 'listen to your breath ebbing and flowing, ebbing and flowing, ebbing and flowing'. This will be your cue to go deep within.

You are using your mind in a more elevated and creative way now. This will serve you in co-creating your own reality.

You and the collective consciousness

—

The collective consciousness is extremely powerful. Time means nothing when you are accessing the field of pure potential. So it doesn't matter when you are reading this book. Whether you read it in 2018 or 2028, it doesn't matter. You can tap into this collective consciousness at any time. In our collective tuning in we sat together and co-created our own peaceful and healing reality with Source Energy. In doing so, know that you are releasing resistance and conjuring up feelings of

'This energy is constantly expanding and rippling out.
Your higher purpose is very much part of an evolved
collective consciousness'

abundance. Through your decision to become a deliberate co-creator, you are co-creating the spark of a positive loop with Source Energy. This will generate huge positive momentum around health, wealth, joy and happiness for you going forward. My wish for you is that this collective tuning in will allow the energy of infinite intelligence to flow undisturbed.

The Mysticism of Co-creation

—

After a little while and some practice something else begins to appear on the horizon. Source Energy is forever expanding. Now you begin to get a faint glimpse of your higher purpose.

The ripples are now reaching out further. You know your connection is there and you are listening to your intuition. The Mysticism of Co-creation opens within you. You are a co-creator with Source Energy and you have been sufficiently badgered by me into acknowledging it. This energy has now gained great momentum. It is beginning to strongly and abundantly ripple out into your life and the lives of all those around you. It brings with it health, wealth, joy and happiness.

As you fulfil your personal purpose, your higher purpose starts to unfold and you move naturally into the broader social dimension. You allow Source Energy to use your talents and gifts to express itself more and more unreservedly.

This energy is constantly expanding and rippling out. Your higher purpose is very much part of an evolved collective consciousness. Everything in the universe has an expanding effect. If you let this energy continue to ripple unrestricted, it will join forces with a collective conscious awareness. At this point huge shifts in awareness are possible and available to you. This shift will ripple out for generations beyond you in many ways that you could never imagine. The effects are limitless.

Transcending the traditional image of God
—

In my working environment with my clients I've seen a big change. People no longer buy into the traditional image of a patriarchal God. This image has become too distorted over time. This distortion has led to many people abandoning the concept of God altogether. Yet somehow people still feel their connection with Source Energy. Perhaps humanity is preparing to leave all the old associations, trials and tribulations of a bygone era behind. Could this be the dawning of a new paradigm shift?

For centuries the equilibrium between women and men has been damaged. We did this with a male version of God. Where the divine and human meet is neither female nor male. A collective human maturity requires a move towards who we really are as individuals first. It requires us to align with Source Energy.

We can call this energy what we like – she, he or it – it really doesn't matter. You know it is within you. You hear it calling you all the time through your intuition. I said in the first chapter that one of the most important characters in this book is *you*. All this is nothing without you. No matter what gender, sexual orientation, religion or race you are, this is all about you and who you really are as an energetic being.

When you consciously align yourself with Source Energy and keep yourself in this alignment, a gradual transformation of consciousness

'No matter what gender, sexual orientation, religion or race you
are, this is about who you really are as an energetic being'

occurs. You are graced with this energy. The more you tune yourself into it, the more abundant your life becomes.

The consolidation of all the principles
—

By using the seven principles in this book in your everyday life, you begin to reprogramme your subconscious mind. Instead of being triggered by old learned behavioural patterns, you form new, positive patterns and these become your immediate response. Remember, it is like learning to drive a car – the more you practice the better you get at it, until one day you just jump into the car and drive off without even thinking about it.

Before I finish I will remind you of the principles and a step-by-step quick-fix process you can use when faced with any of life's tribulations.

1 CONNECT TO SOURCE ENERGY

The first step is to open yourself fully to Source Energy. One of the main things you can do each day is to remind yourself of who you really are. You are magnificent, limitless and infinitely intelligent. You are Source Energy. You have no choice in being the embodiment of this energy because without it you simply wouldn't exist.

Warning: You have a choice whether you want to express your true essence or not, to pinch yourself off from it or to let it flow. Your choice is to turn towards this powerful energy and use it, or ignore it and run from it in fear and in doing so run from your own potential.

Practice: Wake up each morning and remind yourself of 'who you really are'. Try to do a daily meditation, preferably in the morning for at least 15–20 minutes.

2 ALIGNMENT

The second step is to align your mind with the one-mind of Source Energy. This is done by forming an intimate relationship with your own inner child. Your alignment with Source Energy gives you access to the field of pure potential.

Warning: Tuning out keeps you from creating your reality in positivity and awareness.

Practice: Put your hand on your heart and connect with your inner child. Your inner child represents your subconscious mind. When your inner child is triggered and feels afraid, angry or negative in any way, comfort her. Remember visualisation and imagination are excellent tools to connect with your subconscious mind. Your subconscious mind loves a feeling, and every few seconds you are programming it with negative or positive chat. Every 66 days, you form or reiterate a programme in your mind.

3 FEELING AND KNOWING

Your feeling and knowing are extremely important. If you are feeling a lot of positivity, you will create positive loops and your creations will be positively based. Your intuition is constantly calling you; it is the voice of Source Energy. Listen to your intuition.

Warning: If you are creating negative loops and feeling a lot of negativity, your creations will be negatively based.

Practice: Ask your inner child for clarity on any issue you like. Ask for this clarity quickly and easily. Then listen to her, and, most importantly, *act* on your intuition. If you are fearful of acting on your intuition then place your hand on your heart and comfort your fearful inner child as you move forwards, step by step. Remember, your inner child represents your subconscious mind. This holds all knowledge and all memories both positive and negative. Within you lie all the answers.

4 DECISIONS AND EXPECTATIONS

Now it is time to make your *f*ck it* decisions. You are the main character in your life. This character can play any part you want. You decide. You can be healthy, happy, rich, glamorous, successful, a civil rights activist, writer, business owner, rock star – the list goes on.

Warning: Or you can be in lack on all levels, sad, angry and negative. The choice is yours. Your decisions will help you pick the part you really want your character to play.

Practice: Observe your behaviour daily: thought, word and deed. Make clear *f*ck it* decisions often about the big things in your life and the small things.

5 MOMENTUM

After you make your decisions, it's time to step through your fears and create momentum. Igniting only the positive sparks and fuelling them is how you gain positive momentum.

Warning: Igniting only negative sparks and fuelling them as they ignite is how you gain negative momentum. Stop-start momentum does exactly that.

Practice: Observe daily what kind of momentum you are creating around certain situations and people. Ask yourself if this is positive, negative or stop-start momentum. Then actively choose to create more positive momentum.

6 RECEIVING

Ask and you shall receive. There is no limit to what we can receive.

Warning: There is *also* no limit to how you can block yourself from receiving.

Practice: Ask your inner child daily for clarity around your desires. Then listen to your intuition and when you receive the intuition, *act* upon it.

7 RETURN TO SOURCE ENERGY

When you consciously align yourself with Source Energy and keep yourself in this alignment, a gradual transformation of consciousness occurs. You are graced with this energy. The more you tune yourself in to it, the more abundant your life becomes.

Warning: None. You can't get it wrong when you are aligned with Source Energy.

DAILY PRACTICE

1 As you wake up each morning, connect with your inner child and tell her you love her.

2 Meditate for 15–20 minutes to align yourself.

3 After meditation, direct your inner child. Tell her what you want her to do today.

4 Throughout the day, observe yourself. Comfort the child when she is triggered and needs you.

5 Ask your inner child for clarity on whatever you wish for. Remind this inner child of yours that you want the clarity quickly and easily.

6 Listen to your intuition and *act* upon it.

7 Appreciate all you receive.

You now have all the tools you require to create your own wonderful reality, so get going and enjoy, as it is a fantastic journey. But it doesn't end there; in fact it never ends. Source Energy is limitless.

Continue using your diary pages and journal
—

Every night, dip in and out of this book and your journal, asking yourself a few of the questions below. I understand you are tired, but this time is for you and nobody else. Know what you are doing: you are impressing positivity on your subconscious mind. You are aligning yourself with Source Energy and each night you will create positive feelings and momentum just before you go to sleep, which is so important. Write your answers in your journal if you can. Randomly pick a page in this book – any page, it doesn't matter. Read a paragraph before you go to sleep and trust that the information you have received is helping you to deliberately create your own reality. While you are doing this, have your candle lit and put some of your essential oils on. Just before you turn the light off, take a look at a picture of yourself as a child or visualise yourself at a young age. Tell her you love her and you are looking after her.

TOOLBOX

Use your daily practice routine

Continue using your journal

Practice tuning in on your own, or pick a tuning in and repeat it

Meditate every day

Daily affirmations

DIARY PAGES

Each night pick a question or two. There is no right or wrong way to do this.

1 Write down what your intuition was telling you today. Did you listen to it? If so, what happened? Did you ignore it? If so, why?

....

....

....

....

....

2 What has rippled out from you today? Were you rippling out negativity, anger or fear? Were you overwhelmed, irritable and cross, or were you calm, relaxed and happy? Do not judge yourself, you are doing your best.

....

....

....

....

....

....

3 Have a look at what kites you have pulled in today. Even something you feel may not be relevant, for example, buying a new kitchen table. This kite could lead you to having more friends over, company, happiness or even a lover! Everything leads to something else.

....

....

....

....

....

....

....

....

4 Now look at your kites and see what type of momentum you are creating around each one. Is it positive, negative or stop-start momentum?

....

....

....

....

....

....

....

....

....

5 Have you reminded yourself of your *f*ck it* decisions today? These impress on your subconscious mind, so remind yourself daily. *F*ck it*, I have decided to be healthy, wealthy and live in joy and happiness for the rest of my life.

....

....

....

....

....

....

....

....

6 Write a paragraph on all you appreciate about yourself and your life today, including all that you have received today. Starting with your breath.

....

....

....

....

....

....

....

....

7 Did you use any of the tools in your toolbox? Write down what tools you used and make a mental note to use them a little bit more tomorrow.

....

....

....

....

....

....

....

....

....

....

....

....

....

....

....

....

....

Well done, now cosy up and relax ...

Afterword

I will tell you my last little story now. It was a mystical experience which I hold very dear to me. It enhanced deeply my connection with Source Energy. This was freely given to me and I gratefully received it. It has deeply influenced my life.

Many years ago, I was doing a course in Reiki energy healing. These courses weren't as popular back then as they are now. Ireland was still very conservative and closed when it came to energy work. The woman giving the course was elderly, and had been a nun for much of her life. For whatever reason, she had left and was now supporting herself through her healing work. I was a rookie and I was very young. But I had found my niche. I had been naturally doing this for years, but hadn't consciously realised. I took to this energy work like a duck to water and I loved it.

One evening I sat in meditation with this wonderful woman and another woman who was also a nun. That particular night there were only the three of us: two very elderly women and one young woman sitting around a candle in a semi-darkened room. It was a poignant scene, to say the least.

The feeling of peace and tranquillity between the three of us was tangible. We sat in a small circle and began. All I can remember was going really deeply into the meditation. Much like Andrew's experience in Bali, I too was overcome with a deep sense of that same unconditional love. But I also saw an image and felt a very powerful presence. I knew instantly it was Jesus. This was incredibly strong and I just wanted to stay in that energy, as the feeling was so all-encompassing. When I opened my eyes I could see vividly the auric fields around the two other people in the room. This was the first time I had seen the colours around people and it was wonderful. In amazement I told them how vibrant the energy was that surrounded them. It was so beautiful. They could see by my expression that I was totally awestruck by what had happened to me, and they asked me to explain.

I was a little put off telling them that I saw the image of what I felt was Jesus, not to mention telling them that I felt a powerful presence, because I really did think they would be shocked and throw me out. You have to remember all this was extremely new to me. Also I was concerned they would think, 'Who does she think she is?', and that I had an overly inflated ego. But I was so flabbergasted by my experience and very curious to know and gain some understanding around it that I began to timidly recount what I had felt and seen. I couldn't figure out why I would see an image of Jesus. Yes, I had been brought up as a Catholic but Jesus wasn't my 'go to' person in the spiritual world. I have always deemed myself spiritual rather than anything else. So it didn't make much sense to me. I decided to be brave and ask the nuns, thinking they were probably more versed on this subject than I was.

I was right; they were more versed. I was relieved that they were so open. They seemed to understand completely and could explain to me what had happened. I asked them why I would get the image and sense of Jesus. In their explanation, they used the term 'God', but I prefer to go beyond this imagery and use 'Source Energy' instead. They said to me 'Source Energy will always appear to you in the way you will understand it.' This made absolute sense to me. If I had seen one of my relations who had passed on, it would have meant something entirely different. But I had seen what I perceived to be Jesus and as a child I had always associated Jesus with God. Like I said earlier, when I was small I always went straight to god. But in my mind as a child, I did associate Jesus with being God's son.

Those lovely women explained that if Source Energy was going to make itself known to me, it would be through an image that I would understand. As I had no preconceived image of God in my head, Source Energy just had to use the image of Jesus. I learned a big lesson that night. Those two nuns taught me that this infinite intelligence makes itself known to us in all sorts of wonderful ways. Ways that we will be able to comprehend. If I had been familiar with Allah, Buddha, Brahman or Yahweh, Source Energy would have used one of those images instead. It taught me that it doesn't matter what name we have for god. There is only one Source Energy. It is infinitely intelligent and will communicate to you in all sorts of wonderful ways. Much like children, we are given the knowledge in a way we can understand. Those two elderly women were wisely guiding me that night and it is something I will never forget.

This story and all the stories in this book have been shared with you unconditionally with love.

Judith

Further Reading

Chopra, Deepak and Simon, David, *The Seven Spiritual Laws of Yoga*, Wiley, 2005.

Dyer, Wayne, *There is a Spiritual Solution to Every Problem*, Quill, 2003.

Judith, Anodea, *Eastern Body Western Mind*, Celestial Arts, 2004.

Knitter, Paul, *Introducing Theologies of Religions*, Orbis, 2002.

O'Donohue, John, *Anam Cara Spiritual Wisdom from the Celtic World*, Bantam, 1999.

Panikkar, Raimon, *The Cosmotheandric Experience: Emerging Religious Consciousness*, Orbis, 1993.

Rohr, Richard, *Immortal Diamond*, Jossey-Bass, 2013.

Shinn, Florence Scovel, *The Game of Life and How to Play It*, Martino, 2011.

The Three Initiates, *The Kybalion*, available online.